The Seduction of the Church

The Seduction of the Church

*How the Concern to Create
Gender-Neutral Language in Bible and Song
Is Being Misused to Betray Members' Faith*

MALCOLM C. DOUBLES

WIPF & STOCK · Eugene, Oregon

THE SEDUCTION OF THE CHURCH
How the Concern to Create Gender-Neutral Language in Bible and Song Is Being Misused to Betray Members' Faith

Copyright © 2010 Malcolm C. Doubles. All rights reserved. Except for brief quotations in critical publications or reviews, no part of this book may be reproduced in any manner without prior written permission from the publisher. Write: Permissions, Wipf and Stock Publishers, 199 W. 8th Ave., Suite 3, Eugene, OR 97401.

Wipf & Stock
An Imprint of Wipf and Stock Publishers
199 W. 8th Ave., Suite 3
Eugene, OR 97401
www.wipfandstock.com

ISBN 13: 978-1-60899-462-5

Manufactured in the U.S.A.

Permission to quote from Peggy McIntosh's paper, "White Privilege: Unpacking the Invisible Knapsack," has been granted by the author.

Permission to quote from Julia Penelope, *Speaking Freely: Unlearning the Lies of the Fathers' Tongues*, copyright © 1990, has been granted by the author.

Permission to quote from Kathryn Roberts's article, "Our Eyes Will See the Beauty of the King: The Esthetics of Kingship," has been granted by the publisher, *Word & World*.

Permission to quote from Sheldon Sorge's article, "Don't Mess with my Music," has been granted by the publisher, *Presbyterians Today*.

Verse 5 of *Fairest Lord Jesus* as composed by Christoph Dalitz was published under the Creative Commons Attribution-Share Alike 3.0 German License, which explicitly permits copying, distribution, and performance of the music, with the only imposed condition being that works are to be published under the same license again.
Hymn texts otherwise quoted are all in the public domain, with the exception of *Beautiful Jesus*, by Madeleine Forell Marshall, which appears with permission of the author.

Scripture quotations contained herein from the New Revised Standard Version Bible, copyright © 1989, by the Division of Christian Education of the National Council of Churches of Christ in the U.S.A., are used by permission. All rights reserved.

Scripture quotations contained herein from the Revised Standard Version Bible, copyright © 1965, by the Division of Christian Education of the National Council of Churches of Christ in the U.S.A., are used by permission. All rights reserved.

Scripture taken from the New King James Version. Copyright © 1979, 1980, 1982 by Thomas Nelson, Inc. Used by permission. All rights reserved.

Scripture quotations marked (CEV) are from the Contemporary English Version. Copyright © 1991, 1992, 1995 by American Bible Society. Used by Permission. Scripture quotations marked (GNB) are from the Good News Bible. Copyright © 1966, 1971, 1976 by American Bible Society. Used by permission.

Scripture quotations marked (NIV) are taken from the HOLY BIBLE, NEW INTERNATIONAL VERSION®. Copyright © 1973, 1978, 1984 by International Bible Society. Used by permission of Zondervan. All rights reserved.

Scripture quotations marked (NLT) are taken from the *Holy Bible*, New Living Translation, copyright © 1996. Used by permission of Tyndale House Publishers, Inc., Wheaton, Illinois 60189. All rights reserved.

Josephus quotation reprinted by permission of the publishers and Trustees of the Loeb Classical Library from Josephus: Volume IV, Jewish Antiquities, Loeb Classical Library Volume 242, translated by H. St. J. Thackeray, pp. 631–633. Cambridge, MA: Harvard University Press, Copyright © 1930 by the President and Fellows of Harvard College. Loeb Classical Library ® is a registered trademark of the President and Fellows of Harvard College.

To the memory of William H. Schutt (1908–1972),
Organist-Choirmaster and Minister of Music of Richmond, Virginia's
Grace Covenant Presbyterian Church, 1939–1972;

loving husband, devoted father, World War II army veteran,
consummate musician, dedicated churchman, teacher and mentor,
one of the greatest of "the Greatest Generation."

Contents

List of Tables xi
Foreword xiii
Preface xv
Acknowledgments xix

1 Introduction 1

PART ONE   GENDER-NEUTRAL LANGUAGE IN THE BIBLE

2 God Talk 15

3 How to Handle Adam 27

4 The Son of Man 37

5 Impersonality in Psalms and Proverbs 45

6 O Brother, Who Art Thou? 53

PART TWO   GENDER-NEUTRAL LANGUAGE IN SONG

7 Beautiful Savior 65
   Addendum   *Schönster Herr Jesu* 74

8 Hymn of Joy 75
   Addendum A   Handwritten Copy 82
   Addendum B   Proof Copy 84

9 The God of Abraham Praise 87
   Addendum A   Olivers' Twelve Verses 96
   Addendum B   Landsberg/Mann Version 98

10 Make Love Not War 99
    Addendum A   *Soldiers of Christ, Arise* 106
    Addendum B   *Stand Up, Stand Up for Jesus* 108
    Addendum C   *Am I a Soldier of the Cross?* 109

11 What's with Our Christmas Carols? 111
    Addendum   *Stille Nacht* and *Silent Night* 122

12 Praise, My Soul, the King (God) of Heaven 125

13 Conclusion 135

Bibliography 145
Hymn Index 149
Scripture Index 151
Index of Personal Names 155

List of Tables

Table 1. Sample Table Layout	11
Table 2. Genesis 19:17	16
Table 3. I Samuel 16:6	17
Table 4. Deuteronomy 34:5–6	18
Table 5. John 14:26	23
Table 6. Genesis 1:26a–27	28
Table 7. Genesis 2:7, 23b–24a, 25a	30
Table 8. I Corinthians 15:21	33
Table 9. Galatians 3:7 & 9	34
Table 10. Psalm 8:4	37
Table 11. Hebrews 2:6–7	38
Table 12. Daniel 7:13–14	40
Table 13. Matthew 25:31	41
Table 14. Psalm 1:1–3	46
Table 15. Psalm 94:11	49
Table 16. Proverbs 16:9	50
Table 17. Leviticus 19:17–18	54
Table 18. I Corinthians 6:5–6	56
Table 19. Luke 17:3	57
Table 20. Romans 8:29	60
Table 21. Galatians 1:2, 11; 2:4	61
Table 22. Olivers' *The God of Abraham, Praise*	90–91
Table 23. Lutheran Hymnal's Changes to Olivers' Original	95

Foreword

ONE MIGHT EXPECT THAT the subject of gender-inclusive language, sound theology, and the latter's appropriate formulation in gender-neutral language would call for a treatment that is seriously academic. The reader approaching this work with that expectation, however, may be disappointed. What follows is written for the general reader, lacking many of the accouterments usually associated with academic writing. There are but a dozen or so footnotes in the entire work, the average sentence is only about seventeen words in length, the language is non-technical, and almost every reference is immediately available to the ordinary church member. The treatment of the subject, nevertheless, is a serious one.

This work assumes that church members are interested in what is happening with their churches. It also assumes that they have noticed various changes in the language being used to express their faith and have an interest in investigating these changes. The treatment herein is not that of an unconcerned academic, however, but rather the *cri de coeur* of one who loves the church and is genuinely committed to the practice of using gender-inclusive language but at the same time is horrified over the torturous English associated with the implementation of this practice in our mainline churches. Some of this language is so carelessly formulated that it changes the very definition of the faith, the consequences of which can only be tragic.

It is with genuine concern over this issue and its implications for our faith that I invite your attention to what is written herein. Thank you for the time you invest in your investigation of the subject.

Malcolm C. Doubles, 2010

Preface

THIS WORK BEGAN AS a simple exercise to examine the language associated with the elimination of gender-offensive terms in the Bible and in the hymns of the church. As I presented my findings to groups and individuals, however, the nature of the task became more serious and my concerns changed. Eventually I reached the conclusion reached in the final chapter of this work: in their concern to support the use of gender-inclusive language in Scripture, liturgy, and song, many church leaders are unwittingly lending their support to those whose aim is to change the historic Christian faith. This is a betrayal of its members' faith. You are invited to consider the route I followed to reach this conclusion as I detail it in this preface.

Like most raised in the church, I have been exposed to the hymns of the faith since birth. As a child, I participated in the children's choirs of our church, graduating in due course to its youth choirs. I continued to sing in college and seminary and, in my beginning ministry in a home mission pastorate, led the congregational singing, there being no choir to do so and I being the only person "up front." As a college faculty member, I have enjoyed singing in the adult choir of our local church. The result of all this has been, of course, that I have committed to memory parts of many of the hymns as well as important portions of the Bible. Consequently, I noticed the changes in both hymns and Bible as newer versions began to appear in the 1980s and thereafter. For many years, these served simply as a source of amusement whereby fellow basses in the choir could sing older words instead of the newer inclusive language, to the discomfiture of others around us and the despair of our director.

These experiences gave me an idea five or six years ago for a paper to read at a meeting of the Hartsville Discussion Club. Founded in the 1930s and meeting six times annually, this club has eighteen members, each of whom is expected to deliver a paper once every three years. I prepared a paper entitled "Thoughts on the Use of Gender-Neutral

Language in Bible and Song" and presented it at the dinner meeting on October 3, 2005. It seemed to strike a chord and generated a response much more supportive than I had expected. Clearly, some were feeling both frustrated and agitated over many of the changes.

The intensity of the response at the Discussion Club led me to begin work on a monograph on the subject. During the 2006 Christmas break, I shared a preliminary draft of this monograph with an artist friend, Maggie McMahon, UC Foundation Professor of Art at the University of Tennessee-Chattanooga, who offered a number of helpful criticisms and suggestions. After incorporating these, I was forced to put the work aside and turn to another matter full time, that of writing the centennial history of Coker College. Upon the completion of that project and its publication in 2008, I was able to resume my work on gender-inclusive language, although it was considerably limited as my wife and I had to concern ourselves with our move to a continuing care retirement center in December of that same year.

In early April of 2009, I learned that the papers of Henry van Dyke were at the library of Princeton University. He wrote the words of *Joyful, Joyful, We Adore Thee*, one of the hymns I include in my study. Seeking to unravel several curiosities associated with the original text of this hymn, I wrote the library and late the following month received a letter from Deborah Cordonnier of the General and Reference Division of the University's Firestone Library, to whom my initial letter had ultimately been directed. She expended considerable time and energy researching the origins of the poem as well as its publication history. Any contributions to scholarship found in my eighth chapter, devoted to this hymn, are the result of her labors; she should be given the credit, and I certainly give her my thanks.

By the summer of 2009, I had two copies of the first draft of a book-length manuscript ready to share. One copy went to Hartsville, South Carolina's First Presbyterian Church Minister of Music Anna White Hill, my dear friend and the long-suffering choir director who put up with my shenanigans. Anna is one of the most respected choral directors in South Carolina and I felt the need of a musician's opinion, given the extent of commentary about hymns in my work. She went through the work with considerable care, finally concluding that she was convinced by my arguments. I was greatly relieved at this.

I shared the other copy with another long-time friend, the Rev. Dr. Richard Ray, former editor of the John Knox Press and a fellow doctoral alumnus of Scotland's University of St. Andrews. Dick responded to my work with enthusiasm, helping me to see that my concern with matters of language usage had significant theological implications and urging me to broaden my discussion to include a greater emphasis on these issues. He shared copious notes on my work with me and his excitement was contagious. In addition, he encouraged me to take my work to the next meeting of The Society of Biblical Literature (SBL), where I could show it to publishers and seek an outlet for it.

Dick also urged me to submit a chapter suitably edited to the Rev. Ms. Susan Cyre, Executive Director and Editor of *Theology Matters*. I did so, only to be informed that the journal's publication schedule was already set for the next year or so. She was most encouraging about my project, however, and free with her suggestions. Among them was the recommendation that I distinguish more clearly between gender-specific language about God and about humankind. It is to her that I owe thanks for the impetus to develop the chapter entitled "God Talk."

By November 2009, I felt sufficiently comfortable with the manuscript's development to take it to the SBL meeting, where I made contact with a number of publishers. There seemed to be considerable interest among them in the subject and I left copies of the manuscript with three and a CD-ROM of it with a fourth. In addition, I shared an outline of the work with a number of others, many of whom responded later in an encouraging manner. This publication by Wipf and Stock Publishers is the result, one that I hope will be enlightening as well as provocative. I will be especially gratified should it succeed in initiating a movement to change some of the ways those in positions of church leadership have been addressing the issue of the removal of gender-specific language in Scripture, in song, and in services of worship.

Laurinburg, NC. April, 2010
M.C.D.

Acknowledgments

ONE OF THE JOYS of completing any manuscript is taking the opportunity to thank those whose contributions have made a difference in the work. Were it not for the support and suggestions of those identified below, this work might never have been completed and, if finished, would have been much less effective than it now is.

Half of this work is devoted to the hymns of the church, and I owe a great debt of gratitude to those Hartsville churches that allowed me to borrow copies of their latest hymnals. In alphabetical order, these churches are: First Baptist Church, First Presbyterian Church, Our Shepherd Lutheran Church, St. Bartholomew's Episcopal Church, and Wesley United Methodist Church. I kept the hymnals longer than expected, so I am doubly grateful.

Several groups have heard me speak on the subject, and their comments have made their way into the work. The Hartsville Discussion Club heard my first attempt, while the Scotland County, North Carolina, Presbyterian Ministers' Group listened to my conclusions and rendered trenchant comments. Likewise, Dr. Dan Ott's class in Religion and Feminine Issues at St. Andrews Presbyterian College graciously listened to me, questioned me, and commented on my ideas.

I want to thank individuals who read drafts of my work or whose research contributed to it. Sue Cyre, Anna White Hill, Maggie McMahon, and Dick Ray read all or part of my work and made helpful suggestions. Deborah Cordonnier contributed important information I could not have obtained otherwise. I especially appreciate my cousins Jim and Jan Slusser's willingness to share information from their experiences with her book. Last, but not least, my wife Jacque patiently read every word, sometimes more than once, all the while putting up with my distracted presence when I was with her physically but mentally working out some issue associated with this work.

Finally, I would thank the editors who have helped me hammer out this final product. Florence Gilkeson introduced me to a fine editor, Mary Novitsky, who has done yeoman service as the copy editor for this work and I am grateful for her careful eye. Chris Spinks and Christian Amondson of Wipf and Stock have been very supportive of my efforts and prompt to answer my every question.

After all of them are acknowledged, however, I have written what follows and any errors or weaknesses that detract from their contributions must be laid at my door with my apology.

Malcolm C. Doubles, 2010

1

Introduction

SOME YEARS AGO, I was surprised when singing one of my favorite hymns, Harry Emerson Fosdick's *God of Grace and God of Glory*, that as I sang from memory in verse four,

> Gird our lives that they may be
> Armored with all Christ like graces
> In the fight to set men free,

the hymnal read,

> Gird our lives that they may be
> Armored with all Christ like graces,
> Pledged to set all captives free.

Then I began to notice similar changes in a lot of hymns. In addition, the reading of the recently introduced *New Revised Standard Version* (NRSV) of the Bible sometimes sounded peculiar. About the same time, I became conscious of strange, almost non-native, English being used in church liturgy and speech, as pronouns disappeared from language about God. As I examined what was happening, however, I concluded that these changes were more than simple efforts to eliminate gender-specific language. Instead, I began to think that the historical Christian faith itself was under attack, but I could see little to do about it myself, as no one seemed particularly interested in matters of language.

I changed my mind when language issues were recently catapulted onto the public stage with the 2004 publication of Lynne Truss' best-selling book, *Eats, Shoots & Leaves*.[1] Suddenly, matters like comma placement and grammatical structure became worthy topics of conversation and even sources for jokes. I would point out, then, that in any

---

1. Truss, *Eats, Shoots & Leaves*, i.

consideration of language, choice of vocabulary exists as an essential element. Furthermore, the ways people choose words about gender have become increasingly divisive. In what follows, I will address the religious significance of some of the verbal choices made when talking about gender, as well as the changing theology being masked by them in some contemporary translations of the Bible and in the lyrics of many of the hymns we sing.

Ours is a generation that has already incorporated into its educational system an awareness of the power of particular words. For instance, hosts of students around the country now exit secondary school never having encountered any works by Mark Twain, our nation's preeminent raconteur of nineteenth-century America. But after all, his use of the "N-word" in both *Tom Sawyer* and *Huckleberry Finn* makes him an unsuitable author for today's impressionable youth. *Life on the Mississippi*, then, with all that it teaches about the need for better relations between the races and about our nation's roots, as well as Twain's other works, have remained closed books now to several generations of high school graduates. Although the "N-word" does not appear in the Bible or in the church's hymnody, many claim that the continued use of masculine-specific words to make gender-neutral references evokes similar negative responses in some readers. And while schools can ignore Mark Twain, churches cannot ignore the Bible or the great hymns of the faith.

In addition, we must note that human beings are only able to intellectually analyze and process those thoughts that can be effectively communicated with words. Art and music may be able to express ideas that cannot be verbalized, but even discourse about art or music is trapped in the "package" of language. Therefore, if language itself assumes a certain ideological or cultural perspective, ideas discussed with that language automatically ground themselves in those same perspectives.

I like to illustrate this truth with the story told by a linguist friend of mine who, in the late 1940s, spent a sabbatical year in Germany. This was a time when the backyard swimming pool was appearing there. Now, German has a perfectly good word for swimming pool, "die Badeanstalt," but the German people called these new pools, "die Swimmingpool," thereby bringing the two English words into German as a single new word. This friend of mine traveled around Germany showing people photographs of such pools and asking what they called them, was regularly told, "die Swimmingpool," and then always asked why they used the article "die," which indicates the feminine gender. He said that invariably the response would be, "What else could it be?" Yet those of us whose birth language is English would say it should have been "das Swimmingpool," that is, neuter, rather than the feminine gender assumed by those whose birth language was German. All of which is simply to note that the structure of a language influences the culture of its native speakers, often in ways beyond their awareness.

The recognition of this helps us understand that the translation of a document involves more than simply word-for-word equivalency from one language to another. When the document under consideration is a sacred text, the urgency of the matter becomes more extreme, as translators wrestle with the cultural challenge imposed by the task of moving with accuracy from one linguistic milieu to another. The Jewish community attempted to address this issue by retaining the reading of the original Hebrew language in its synagogue services and providing a verse-by-verse translation into the vernacular, a practice which can be attested at least as early as the time of Jesus. Christians, on the other hand, faced with an original biblical text in three languages, Hebrew, Aramaic, and Greek, have never seriously considered this option, having chosen instead to rely entirely upon translations. What happens in these translations, therefore, is of great importance to believers as they study the words of these Scriptures and sing hymns based upon them.

As far as gender-inclusive language is concerned, Julia Penelope addresses the issue with these words in her book, *Speaking Freely: Unlearning the Lies of the Fathers' Tongues*:

> Understanding how the structure of English controls the way we think and act is crucial to our welfare . . . Words hurt us, but languages are much more than the words in their vocabularies. They are systems of rules, rules which speakers find useful for saying what they want to say . . . English does more than hinder and hurt women; it proscribes the boundaries of the lives we might imagine ourselves to live.[2]

And Christian religious language in English is particularly onerous, based as it is on the Bible, which is thoroughly *androcentric*, that is, male centered and oriented. Our hymns, consequently, also reflect this linguistic orientation.

2. Penelope, *Speaking Freely: Unlearning the Lies of the Fathers' Tongues*, xii–xiv.

Furthermore, that more than language skews life in favor of the males of the human species has been increasingly recognized. For the most part, however, men tend to be unaware of their privileges as men, even when they may grant that women are disadvantaged by what has been termed our "patriarchal system." It has been argued that such privilege comprises an invisible package of unearned assets that any man can count on each day, but about which most men are oblivious. Such privilege is "like an invisible weightless knapsack of special provisions, maps, passports, codebooks, visas, clothes, tools, and blank checks."[3] Many of these privileges are unearned, and men tend to be oblivious of them.

It is men and not women who make the most money; men and not women who dominate the government and the corporate boards; men and not women who dominate virtually all of the most powerful positions of society. Furthermore, it is women and not men who suffer the most from intimate violence and rape; women and not men who are the most likely to be poor; women and not men who are, on the whole, given the short end of patriarchy's stick. While men may be harmed by patriarchy, women are oppressed by it.

For instance, a man's odds of being hired when competing for a job against a female applicant are probably skewed in his favor, unless a civil rights quota is at issue, and the more prestigious the job, the larger the odds are skewed. In addition, a man can be confident that his co-workers won't think he got the job because of his sex—even though that might be true! And the decision to hire a man will never be based on assumptions about whether or not he might choose to have a family sometime soon. Finally, the odds of a man's encountering sexual harassment on the job are so low as to be negligible.

If a man seeks political office, his relationship with his children, or whom he hires to take care of them, will probably not be scrutinized by the press. Furthermore, chances are that his elected representatives are mostly people of his own sex, and the more prestigious and powerful the elected position, the more likely this is to be true. A man can be somewhat sure that if he asks to see "the person in charge," he will face a

---

3. McIntosh, "White Privilege: Unpacking the Invisible Knapsack," 1. This article is excerpted from Working Paper 189, "White Privilege and Male Privilege: A Personal Account of Coming to See Correspondences through Work in Women's Studies" (1988), and can be purchased from the Wellesley College Center for Research on Women, Wellesley, MA 02181.

person of his own sex, and the higher up in the organization the person is, the surer he can be, testimony to the continuing presence of the so-called "glass ceiling."

As a child, the chances are that a boy was encouraged to be more active and outgoing than his sisters. In addition, he would not have been taught to fear walking alone after dark in average public spaces. Beyond that, a boy could choose from an almost infinite variety of children's media featuring positive, active, non-stereotyped heroes of his own sex. Nor did he ever have to look for it: male heroes were the default. Throughout childhood, adolescence, and adulthood, a male can turn on the television or glance at the front page of the newspaper and see people of his own sex widely represented, every day, without exception.

Finally, a man can be confident that the ordinary language of day-to-day existence will always include his sex. "All men are created equal," mailman, chairman, freshman, he. In all of this, a man has the privilege of being unaware of his male privilege. Unfortunately, denials that amount to taboos often surround the subject of advantages that men gain from women's disadvantages. These denials protect male privilege from being fully acknowledged, lessened, or ended. They instead perpetuate the unearned privileges and advantages enjoyed by men in our society.

The difference between earned and unearned privilege or advantage can be seen in a consideration of my interest in the subject of this book, of which the first half involves a study of biblical material. Inasmuch as I have studied under and worked with some of the world's most widely acclaimed biblical scholars and hold the PhD degree in Biblical Criticism from Scotland's University of St. Andrews, I have earned the privilege to speak with some authority on matters biblical. However, to the extent that respect is given my views simply because I am a man, then my positions are being accorded an unearned advantage.

In what follows, I write a lot about language, both its use and misuse, a subject on which I have earned the privilege of speaking. I majored in English in college, studied for a year as a graduate student at the French-speaking faculté de théologie protestante in Montpellier, France, worked as one of the translator/revisers engaged by T & T Clark publishers to render the "new" Schürer into English from its original German, taught Latin at the secondary school level as well as both Greek and Hebrew at the college level, was the founding Chair of the steering committee for the Association for Targumic and Aramaic Studies, and taught English for three semesters in Shanghai at one of China's "key universities." Although I think I have earned the privilege of speaking about matters of language, to the extent that my words are valued because I am a man, then I am being accorded an unearned privilege.

Half of what follows is devoted to an examination of the hymns of the church and, although I am not a church musician, I have spent a lifetime immersed in its music. I grew up in a church where the choir was a major part of the youth activity, to the extent that as a child I was expected to learn by heart the words and melody of Handel's "Hallelujah Chorus." After my voice changed, I learned the bass of this work and of many others, as well. For over thirty years I have been an officer of a civic choral group whose performances are now broadcast state-wide. For almost my entire life, I have sung in a church choir. For all of these reasons, I believe I have earned the privilege of commenting on the hymn practices of the church. At the same time, one would be granting me unearned privilege to prefer the musical positions I argue over those that might be put forward by the female Minister of Music under whose direction I have been singing for the past thirty years.

Theological issues inform this entire work from first to last, and I think I have earned the privilege to address them. I hold the BD (Bachelor of Divinity) degree, am an ordained Presbyterian clergyman, and served as a church extension pastor for five-and-a-half years, during which time I was the founding minister of two churches. Subsequently, I taught religion at the undergraduate level for many years. For over twenty years I have been a regular instructor at a lay school of theology. By education and profession, I have earned the privilege of speaking about theological matters. To the extent that my views are endorsed because I am a man, however, I will have been accorded an unearned advantage in this discussion of how the implementation of inclusive language principles is being used to change Christian theology. It is worth noting at this point, too, that on this particular subject a man may be at an unearned disadvantage in any discussion of these issues with women!

Finally, I am well aware of the way by which major changes are often begun with almost insignificant moves. Serving for twenty-one years as a college provost and dean of faculty has given me ample opportunity to observe, and even sometimes to initiate, seemingly unimportant changes that later led to major shifts in college curricula and practice. Furthermore, I know that this "for want of a horseshoe a kingdom is lost" manner of change is not restricted to the college world, but is familiar to anyone who has had managerial responsibilities, worked teaching young people, or raised a family. Such experiences have earned me the advantage of being able to speak about the potential implications of the changes I will be identifying in the rest of this book. At the same time, to the extent that my concerns are considered valid because I am a man expressing them, then just to that extent have I been granted unearned and undeserved privilege.

Although much has been done in recent decades to address this issue of unearned privilege, much remains to be done. Civil rights legislation has served to make illegal overt discrimination against minorities, including women. At the same time, more subtle issues have also been addressed. Among these more subtle issues are those about gender-neutral language. It is now time to turn to that subject, especially as it has impacted life in the mainline Protestant churches.

Gender-neutral language as a style of writing was first proposed by feminist language reformers in universities and seminaries during the 1970s, and has been accepted as normative in many schools and publications since about 1980. As a result, a generation of seminarians has entered the pulpit almost traumatized over the issue of "God-talk," unable to use the personal pronoun "he" to refer to the Divine, and understandably unwilling to use "she," although in some circles the feminine pronoun for God is beginning to be entertained.

This ambivalence impacts public worship in various ways, including Calls to Worship such as the following that I experienced recently:

Leader: Thank God! Pray to God by name! Tell everyone you meet what God has done!
People: Sing God songs, belt out hymns, translate God's wonders into music!
Leader: Honor God's holy name with Hallelujahs, you who seek God. Live a happy life.
People: Keep your eyes open for God, watch for God's works.
Leader: Be alert for signs of God's presence.
All: Remember the world of wonders God has made.[4]

One could at least hope for synonyms to appear, perhaps "the Lord," "the Divine," or "the Almighty," but all we get is the word "God" repeated eleven times within nine short lines. Unimaginative and non-native lan-

---

4. August 10, 2008, at a church I prefer to leave unidentified.

guage of this sort invites both scorn and bewilderment, so our increasingly empty pews need not be a surprise.

Sometimes, however, the careless use of synonyms to avoid such repetitive language can create theological confusion. For instance, the following Call to Worship appeared in the bulletin of another church recently:

> One: Ascribe to the Lord glory and strength. Ascribe to the Lord the glory of God's name.
> All: Worship the Lord in holy splendor.
> One: May the Lord give strength to God's people!
> All: May the Lord bless God's people with peace![5]

In this case, there are no pronouns, thereby inviting the reader to raise questions about antecedents. Are "the Lord" and "God" identical, and thus synonyms? Or are we talking about two different beings, "the Lord" being one and "God" the other?

For those accustomed to the "God-language" of the church, this is probably not a problem. On the other hand, evangelism assumes an attempt to reach out to the unchurched, which includes those unfamiliar with the usual language of worship. Inasmuch as contemporary attempts at gender neutrality have produced such unintended but confusing consequences within the language of worship, one can only hope that its results in Bible and in song have been more fruitful, given the importance of addressing the issue of male privilege.

The first church-wide attempt to reflect gender inclusiveness was the Inclusive Language Lectionary published by the National Council of Churches in 1983. A lectionary lists the Bible readings for church services during the year, and this one proposed by the NCC in 1983 presented gender-neutral adaptations of Scripture for the readings prescribed. At the same time, it excluded Biblical verses advocating the submissiveness of women, like First Corinthians 11:3- 16 and 14:34-35, Ephesians 5:22-24, Colossians 3:18, First Timothy 2:11-15, and First Peter 3:1-6. Not that omissions in lectionaries originated with this concern about sexist talk, however. Lectionaries always pretended to be multi-year, usually three-year, reads through the Bible, but no one ever insisted on including all of Leviticus, with its laws, or the last half of Exodus, with its tabernacle dimensions and worship instructions, or portions of the

---

5. January 11, 2009, and again I'll not identify the church.

Song of Solomon, with its sexually suggestive language. Nevertheless, the Inclusive Language Lectionary of 1983 was the first attempt to practice omissions on the basis of gender considerations.

The *New Jerusalem Bible*, a Roman Catholic version which appeared in 1985, was the first Bible to feature a moderate use of gender-neutral language. The first version of the Bible to use gender-neutral language in a thorough and systematic way, however, was the *New Revised Standard Version* (NRSV), which appeared in 1990. This version was created under a mandate from the copyright holder, the National Council of Churches, to eliminate "sexist" language. As noted on page xii in its preface,

> The mandates from the Division *(of Education and Ministry of the NCC)* specified that, in references to men and women, masculine-oriented language should be eliminated as far as this can be done without altering passages that reflect the historical situation of ancient patriarchal culture.

Thus was another charge added to the normal problems of translation.

In addition to Scripture, music is also an important element in the life of the church. John Calvin, commenting on Psalm 33:2, wrote "that music is very useful for awakening the minds of men and moving their hearts."[6] Music sets the atmosphere of a church service, communicates doctrine through singing, and expresses the believer's view of what God is like. I count myself fortunate to have been raised in Richmond's Grace Covenant Presbyterian Church during the years when the renowned William H. Schutt was Minister of Music. Every child sang in a choir, and as I noted earlier, at least once a year all the choirs joined to sing the "Hallelujah Chorus" from Handel's *Messiah*. Every youth raised in that congregation entered adulthood with the firm conviction that Jesus was "King of Kings and Lord of Lords, and He shall reign forever and ever," the closing words of the chorus. In this same way, the words of the hymns of the church help formulate and crystalize the beliefs of Christian adherents.

Just as modern translations of the Bible have attempted to be gender neutral in their language, so also have recent hymnals reflected this effort. I have used the following denominational editions in this study:

* *Lutheran Book of Worship*—copyrighted in 1979.

* *The Hymnal 1982*—Episcopalian, copyrighted in 1985.

---

6. Calvin, *Psalms*, i, 539.

* *The United Methodist Hymnal*—copyrighted in 1989.
* *The Presbyterian Hymnal*—copyrighted in 1990 and using the NRSV for Bible selections.
* *The Baptist Hymnal*—copyrighted in 1991.
* The New Century Hymnal—United Church of Christ, copyrighted in 1995.

In addition to these recent editions, occasionally I have consulted earlier hymnals, as well.

In both Bible and hymns, gender neutrality is achieved in one of two ways. The simplest is to omit the gender-specific material, whether a word, a phrase, or an entire piece. Where this is not practical, then new words or statements can be developed as substitutes for the offending material, thereby discarding the masculine reference for persons of unspecified gender.

In the body of this work, I shall examine how these two principles have been implemented, using table charts to present biblical translations, thereby facilitating a comparative examination of the different versions. Inasmuch as I am concerned with what is happening in our mainline churches, I use the most recent Authorized Versions, namely the *New Revised Standard Version* and the *Revised Standard Version*, for my primary biblical comparisons. In addition, in my table charts I include the first Authorized Bible, that is, the *King James Version Bible*. Finally, as a matter of interest I also include the *New King James Version*, the versions published by the American Bible Society (the *Good News Bible* and the *Contemporary English Version*), plus the *New International Version* and the *New Language Translation*.

In the tables presenting these various translations, the most recent Authorized Versions appear in the top row. At the same time, the more modern translation of each source is presented in the left column. In this way, my hope is that you the reader will find it relatively simple to compare the earlier versions with those that came later, while also noting the differences that result from our contemporary concern for gender inclusiveness. To save space, I render only the top row fully, abbreviating the other versions to include only the terms under consideration.

NRSV New Revised Standard Version	RSV Revised Standard Version
NKJV New King James Version	KJV King James Version
NLT New Language Translation	NIV New International Version
CEV Contemporary English Version	GNB Good News Bible

To look at our hymns, rather than examine disparate lines from a host of hymns, I devote separate chapters to three popular ones with which we all have some familiarity: *Joyful, Joyful, We Adore Thee*; *The God of Abraham Praise*; and *Fairest Lord Jesus*. In addition, I devote a chapter to our Christmas carols and another to warlike hymns that are no longer sung. Finally, I compare an historic hymn, *Praise, My Soul, the King of Heaven*, with a contemporary version adopted by the Ecumenical Women's Center in 1974.

When you have finished this work, I hope you the reader will agree with me that the issue of gender-neutral language in Bible and song requires more serious attention and much greater sophistication than has been exhibited so far. Furthermore, I hope you will also agree that our legitimate concern about inclusive language has been misused to launch an attack on the faith itself.

PART ONE

Gender-Neutral Language in the Bible

2

God Talk

IN THE REALM OF religious discourse, concerns about gender-neutral language are multiplied. In addition to the usual preference of the English language for masculine words to refer to humanity at large, there is the matter of how to talk about God. Historically, the masculine has been used for "God talk." Although words like *God* and *the Divine* are clearly gender neutral, *Lord*, as in *the Lord*, *Father*, as in *Our Father*, and *King*, as in *the King of heaven*, at least imply the masculine, however vehemently one may argue for the gender-neutral, spiritual nature of the Divine. Parents, leaders, and rulers may be either masculine or feminine, of course, and it is to such concepts that these terms refer, but because each has a feminine corollary, *mother* with *father*, *lady* with *lord*, and *queen* with *king*, it is a simple matter to caricature these terms as masculine only.

Inasmuch as these masculine-oriented terms comprise the language of the Bible as it refers to the Divine, those who would translate it must wrestle with the issue. In the case of the NRSV, the most recent of the Authorized Versions, the gender-inclusiveness mandate seems to have been applied scrupulously in reference to humanity, while most of the language about God appears to have been unaffected. For instance, as the reader begins in Genesis, chapter 1, the term *God* appears over thirty times, while the personal pronoun *he* referring to God appears over a half-dozen times. One ends this chapter confident that the editors of the NRSV have restricted their gender-inclusive language charge to references involving humankind only. Absolute confidence would be misplaced, however, as there are exceptions.

Some of these exceptions can be justified on the basis of readings from other ancient versions. For instance, Genesis 19 tells the story of the depravity of Sodom and the escape of Lot and his family. Verse 16 tells of the men who forcibly ejected Lot, his wife, and his two daughters from the city, "the Lord being merciful to him." In the following verse, they are told to flee and not look back.

Genesis 19:17

NRSV	RSV
When they brought them outside they[a] said, "Flee for your life; do not look back or stop anywhere in the Plain; flee to the hills, or else you will be consumed."	And when they had brought them forth, they[a] said, "Flee for your life; do not look back or stop anywhere in the valley; flee to the hills, lest you be consumed."
NKJV	KJV
So it came to pass, when they had brought them outside, that he said . . .	And it came to pass, when they had brought them forth abroad, that he said . . .
NLT	NIV
"Run for your lives!" the angels warned . . .	. . . one of them said,
CEV	GNB
. . . one of the angels said . . .	Then one of the angels said . . .

[a]Gk Syr Vg: Heb *he*

The Hebrew says that *he said* to flee, where the only possible antecedent is *the Lord* in the previous verse. Since the Greek, Syriac, and Latin Vulgate versions all have readings indicating that one or more of the angels spoke this warning, the NRSV as well as other modern translations avoid the gender-specific *he*, and both the NRSV and the RSV footnote the change to give its source. Although in popular thought God gave Lot and his family the instructions including the one not to look back during their flight, only the NKJV of the modern versions retains such a reading, obviously in deference to the original King James Version. When Lot's wife looks back she is turned into a pillar of salt, the penalty for disobedience regardless of who gave the command.

Occasionally, however, the NRSV editors act to make changes when there is no support from the ancient versions for them. For instance, one of the most widely quoted verses in Genesis appears in chapter 15, where the Lord has called Abram into covenant and promised to make his descendants more numerous than the stars in the night sky. Verse 6 describes Abram's response with these words in the NRSV,

And he believed the Lord; and the Lord reckoned it to him as righteousness,

footnoting the second occurrence of *the Lord* to indicate that the Hebrew says *he*. This verse is cited by both Paul (Galatians 3:6; Romans 4:3) and James (James 2:23) in the New Testament, giving added significance to its importance. Both use it to support their respective positions, Paul that salvation is a matter of faith-righteousness and James that Abram's obedience defined his salvation. Why the NRSV editors should choose to inject a redundancy like *Lord . . . Lord* at this place in the name of gender inclusiveness is a mystery, especially as the Septuagint reads the passive, *it was reckoned*, what is quoted by Paul and James.

This particular redundancy appears elsewhere in the NRSV, as well. In chapter 16 of First Samuel, the story is told of Samuel's search within Jesse's family for a King of Israel to be the successor to Saul. In verse 6, we read the clearly non-native English statement in the NRSV, "Surely the Lord's anointed is now before the Lord." Every teacher of English would require the pronoun in this situation, or else some reworking of the entire statement, like that found in the Contemporary English Version (CEV). Again, the decision of the NRSV editors is a mystery, as presumably proper use of the language should characterize any Authorized Version of Holy Scripture.

I Samuel 16:6

NRSV	RSV
When they came, he looked on Eliab and thought, "Surely the Lord's anointed is now before the Lord."[a]	When they came, he looked on Eliab and thought, "Surely the Lord's anointed is before him."
NKJV	KJV
". . . is before him."	". . . is before him."
NLT	NIV
"Surely this is the Lord's anointed."	"Surely the Lord's anointed stands here before the Lord."
CEV	GNB
"He has to be the one the Lord has chosen," Samuel said to himself.	"This man standing here in the Lord's presence is surely the one he has chosen."

[a]Heb *him*

A seemingly innocuous change at the end of Deuteronomy deserves considerable attention. In Deuteronomy 34:5–6, Moses' death is described in words that had a great impact on developing Jewish thought through the years. As can be seen, in this narrative the RSV, NIV, and NKJV all follow the KJV description of Moses' burial by stating that *he buried him*. By doing so, they translate the Hebrew literally, requiring the reader to identify the antecedent to the personal pronoun *he*. In both languages, Hebrew and English, the only possible antecedent is *the Lord*, and the GNB as well as the CEV acknowledges this by simply starting a new sentence having *The Lord* as its subject. This interment at the hands of the Divine is then emphasized by the final clause of the verse stressing the unknown location of Moses' burial site.

Deuteronomy 34:5–6

NRSV	RSV
Then Moses, the servant of the Lord, died there in the land of Moab, at the Lord's command. He was buried in a valley in the land of Moab, opposite Beth-peor, but no one knows his burial place to this day.	So Moses the servant of the Lord died there in the land of Moab, according to the word of the Lord, and he buried him in the valley in the land of Moab opposite Beth-peor, but no man knows the place of his burial to this day.
NKJV	KJV
... according to the word of the Lord. And He buried him ...	... according to the word of the Lord. And he buried him ...
NLT	NIV
... as the Lord had said. He was buried ...	... as the Lord had said. He buried him ...
CEV	GNB
... as the Lord had said. The Lord buried him ...	... as the Lord had said he would. The Lord buried him ...

In contrast to all these other versions, the NRSV omits any possible pronominal reference to a divine antecedent by placing the verb in the passive voice with Moses as the subject, *He was buried*. In this reading, it follows the suggestion made in the margin of the American Standard

Version of 1901, thereby accepting the argument that the aforesaid antecedent is indefinite, rather than a reference to *the Lord*. As far as gender neutrality is concerned, however, this eliminates one place, at least, where the masculine pronoun is used to refer the Divine, although, as we have noted, in general the NRSV leaves such pronouns undisturbed. At the same time, a new question is injected, to wit, what happened to those who buried Moses? Did they all have memory lapses? Were they all interred with Moses? In other words, a new issue is created for an already difficult narrative.

Unfortunately, by accepting this latter reading, the editors of the NRSV remove the basis for an important development of ideas within Judaism relative to Moses, namely, that Moses was translated at death into heaven. Thus he was understood to be a member of the threesome in the Old Testament who were "alive with God," joining Enoch and Elijah. Of Enoch, it is said in Genesis 5:24,

> Enoch walked with God; then he was no more, because God took him.

And this in a chapter detailing Adam's descendants, about all of whom except Enoch it is said, *and he died*. Of Elijah, reference is only required to the story of the fiery chariot and the prophet's ascent into heaven as described in Second Kings 2:9–12.[1] The understanding of the Old Testament narration of the translation into heaven of these three helps to explain their importance in the New.

As far as Elijah is concerned, one need only consider the end of the Old Testament, where, in its next to last verse, we read,

> Lo, I will send you the prophet Elijah before the great and terrible day of the Lord comes. (Malachi 4:5, NRSV)

Given this expectation, one can appreciate the readiness of some to identify Jesus with Elijah, as noted in the Synoptic Gospel account of Peter's recognition of Jesus as the Christ (Mk 8:20//Mt 16:14//Lk 9:19). Moses and Elijah, however, appear together in the story of the Transfiguration, after this statement by Peter:

---

1. In what follows, I have no intention of joining the debate about Moses' body proposed by Richard Carrier in chapter 5 of his book, *The Empty Tomb*, but I would note that he has injected the subject into the popular domain.

> Six days later, Jesus took with him Peter and James and John, and led them up a high mountain apart, by themselves. And he was transfigured before them, and his clothes became dazzling white, such as no one on earth could bleach them. And there appeared to them Elijah with Moses, who were talking with Jesus. (NRSV, Mark 9:2–4)

One important part of the requisite background for this transfiguration event is, of course, the translation of Moses, the possibility for which rests upon the description of his burial as *by the Lord*.

Much of the evidence to support the existence of this belief about Moses among the Jews of Palestine in the time of Jesus no longer exists. There are, however, statements that give strong indications about it. Elsewhere in the New Testament, we read in Jude 9:

> But when the archangel Michael contended with the devil and disputed about the body of Moses, he did not dare to bring a condemnation of slander against him, but said, "The Lord rebuke you!" (NRSV)

a clear reference to Moses' "translation."

From the realm of hellenistic Judaism we read from the long version of *Orphica*, dated sometime between 150 B.C. and A.D. 50:

> Yes he after this is established in the great heaven. . . .
> As the saying of the ancients, as the one water-born has described it,
> The one who received [revelations] from God in aphorisms,
> in the form of a double law.[2]

The *he in the great heaven* is clearly identified as Moses by the *water-born* reference to the bull-rushes, while the *double law* must mean the two tablets of the Ten Commandments.

Furthermore, Josephus, the first-century Jewish historian, writes the following in his *Antiquities*:

> But when he arrived on the mountain called *Abaris*, . . . he dismissed the elders. And, while he bade farewell to Eleazar and Joshua and was yet communing with them, a cloud of a sudden descended upon him and he disappeared in a ravine. But he has written of himself in the sacred books that he died, for fear lest

---

2. Charlesworth, *Pseudepighrapha*, ii; 800.

they should venture to say that by reason of his surpassing virtue he had gone back to the Deity.[3]

That Josephus thinks it necessary to describe the translation of Moses as "he had gone back to the Deity" is a clear indication that he knew of those who believed that Moses never died.

There is, therefore, ample evidence to justify the understanding that, among the Jews of Palestine in the time of Jesus, many believed that Moses had been translated, or in other words, been taken directly into heaven at his death. This, then, made it possible for him to accompany Elijah in their meeting with Jesus at the Transfiguration. Unfortunately, the NRSV by reading *he was buried* eliminates the Old Testament basis for this belief and, as a result, makes the understanding of the Transfiguration even more problematical for today's believer, all in the name of trying to avoid a reference to the Lord as *he*.

In addition to the availability of other ancient language versions as well as alternative translations, the omission of terms considered offensive is the most obvious way to create gender-neutral language. One might question the feasability of such a practice when translating the Bible into English, but readers have become accustomed already to encountering such omissions. Improvements in our understanding of the original languages as well as continuing sophistication in the analysis of biblical manuscripts have produced changes in newer translations of Scripture. Sometimes these changes require omissions in the translated text.

For instance, no expression occurs more frequently in the King James Version than that which reads, *and it came to pass*. So often does this occur that the word *pass* is confined to an appendix in *Strong's Concordance*, one of the most widely used works of its type, listing as it does the location by chapter and verse of every occurrence of every word in the King James Version.[4] Because of its relegation to the appendix, appearances of the word "pass" unrelated to this expression are, perforce, ignored. For instance, should you wish to find the account about Moses where, *The Lord passed before him*, as narrated in Exodus 33:19—34:6a, you could only find it by looking under *Lord* in pages 819 to 862 of Strong's work, and even then only the above 34:6 verse with *passed* is recorded. Yet sermons have been preached with *And it came to pass* as

---

3. Josephus, *Jewish Antiquities*, iv. 325–6 (IV/viii/48). See also iii. 96 (III/v/7). Josephus also provides one of the important extra-biblical references to Jesus (xviii. 63*f* and xx. 200).

4. Strong, *Concordance* (1984).

the text, although, with the exception of the New King James Version (NKJV), no recent translations of the Bible anywhere use the statement. And this for a very simple reason related to a better understanding of the language.

The expression, *and it came to pass*, is the way the King James' translators chose to render the Hebrew form *wayehi* (ויהי), which appears over 290 times in the Old Testament.[5] It appears in its Greek form, *kai egeneto* (καὶ ἐγένετο), some 64 times in the New Testament, 46 of these in the Lucan writings, either in his Gospel or in Acts, where it is also translated *and it came to pass* in the King James Version.[6] Contemporary translators simply use *and*, *and so*, *then*, or another conjunction to indicate the continuation of the narrative. In fact, should one wish to make a story sound Biblical in today's speech, it would be enough to simply start it with the words, "and it came to pass." Everyone would think you were telling a Bible story and no one would suspect that you were using an expression that does not even exist in the sacred text! It has disappeared from all modern translations of Scripture, with the exception of the NKJV. That contemporary versions of the Bible omit material found in the King James is no longer a surprise to readers.

When turning to the New Testament, one can find an unfortunate omission in John 14:26. Here the Greek has an example of what grammarians call *casus pendens*, that is, the resumption of the subject or object by the personal pronoun.[7] In this case, we do not have just a personal pronoun, but the demonstrative pronoun (ἐκεῖνος = *ekeinos* = *that one*) in the nominative masculine, therefore usually translated *he*. The NRSV omits the pronoun, again a change made for the sake of good English style which, fortuitously also renders a reading gender neutral. It could, however, have retained the Greek emphasis and style by using *that one* or *this one*. That the translators chose not to do so results in the removal of one of those places in the New Testament where the reader can note the person of the Holy Spirit.

---

5. BDB, 224.

6. Moulton, *Grammar*, ii, 425–428. This form is generally considered to be a Hebraism in the Greek text, thus an indication of Semitic influence on the language of the New Testament narrative.

7. *ibid.*, 424.

John 14:26

NRSV	RSV
But the Advocate,[1] the Holy Spirit, whom the Father will send in my name, will teach you everything, and remind you of all that I have said to you.	But the Counselor, the Holy Spirit, whom the Father will send in my name, he will teach you all things, and bring to your remembrance all that I have said to you.
NKJV	KJV
But the Helper, the Holy Spirit . . . He will teach you all things.	But the Comforter, which is the Holy Spirit . . . he shall teach you . . .
NLT	NIV
But when the Father sends the Counselor . . . —and by the Counselor I mean the holy Spirit—he will teach you . . .	But the Counselor, the Holy Spirit . . . will teach you . . .
CEV	GNB
But the Holy Spirit will come . . . The Spirit will teach . . .	The Helper, the Holy Spirit, . . . will teach you everything . . . .

[1] Or *Helper*

Affirmation of belief in the Trinity as the way to understand the nature of God is fundamental to Christianity, whether in its Orthodox, Roman Catholic, or Protestant formulations. This affirmation found its classical expression in the Nicene Creed, a confession at the heart of the church's worship. As many have noted, however, there are few unambiguously trinitarian statements in the New Testament, and when a verse occurs that permits description of the Spirit in personal terms it should not be ignored, especially in light of some contemporary movements to eliminate trinitarian theology altogether or, alternatively, to rewrite it in feminine terms. In any event, it is unfortunate in the extreme for an Authorized Version of Scripture to reinforce unaware believers today in their bad habit of referring to the Holy Spirit as an *it*, especially when such a rendering is unnecessary.

Advances in our knowledge of the scriptural languages, then, as well as of the texts of both Old and New Testaments have resulted in some omissions occurring in newer versions of the Bible. In addition, the demands of inclusive language related to gender have also prompted occasional omissions. Unfortunately, in certain cases such changes have had negative effects, either in the understanding of later developments in the Bible or in Christian theology.

For the most part, however, the NRSV translators have been very conservative about changing the masculine pronominal references to the Divine. The reader sees this by the Bible's fifth verse, Genesis 1:5, in these words about the very first day of Creation:

> God called the light Day, and the darkness he called Night. And there was evening and there was morning, the first day.

In general, this practice of allowing God to be called *he* or *him* is followed throughout the NRSV. The examples given earlier illustrate the types of problems that can occur when careless attempts are made to be more gender inclusive. It would seem appropriate, then, to ask that future translators of Holy Scripture exercise even greater caution over the potential effects of seemingly innocuous changes in language about God, what we popularly call "God Talk."

Since it is the most recent Authorized Version, therefore the pew Bible in most churches that make up the National Council of Churches, one would expect the NRSV to inform the manner by which the leaders of these same congregations speak of God. A generation of clergy, however, has been apparently overwhelmed by those in the mainline seminaries who, while advocating the Bible as the rule of faith and practice, find themselves unable to follow the Bible's way of speaking about God.

I was stunned recently by a liturgy where First Peter 2:9 was printed this way:

> But you are a chosen race, a royal priesthood, a holy nation, God's own people, in order that you may proclaim the mighty acts of the One who called you out of darkness into God's marvelous light.

A glance at the NRSV pew Bible will reveal to any member of the congregation that the verse as printed in the liturgy has been altered in its last line to substitute *the One* for *him* and *God's* for *his*. What is the unsuspecting believer to think? What is the place of Holy Scripture if the liturgy of the church changes the words of the very Bible put in the pews for the edification of its membership? Who has the right to change the words of the Bible? What words can be changed? Are some sacrosanct?

But back to the liturgy in question. As any native speaker of English knows, the presence of a possessive noun instead of a pronoun in the predicate of a sentence implies an element of distinction between subject and object. In this case, the reader is invited to ask about the difference between *the One* and *God*, thus entertaining an implicit question about the truth of the monotheism of the Christian faith. Had the verse simply been quoted as presented in the NRSV, no such question would exist. Perhaps it is time that churches begin to insist that their leaders use the language of their Authorized Version of Scripture to talk about God. I suspect that most members would appreciate it.

3

How to Handle Adam

THE TRANSLATORS OF THE NRSV may not have exercised themselves over gender-neutral language when talking about God, but the same cannot be said of their treatment of references to humankind, a concept for which English has historically used the word *man*. In both Old and New Testaments, this requires a decision about how to alter the word *man*, since, in general, the Hebrew and the Greek likewise use this word to refer to humankind in general. Gender neutrality calls for special attention at this point.

The Hebrew word *ha-adam* (האדם) is the term translated as *man* and appears about one hundred times in the Old Testament (although seldom in the wisdom literature), while *adam* (אדם) without the definite article *the* (ה) is the name of the first man, Adam. When found with the particle, as in Genesis 2:7, it often means a particular man and may be translated as *the man* or simply *man*.

Alternatively, as in Genesis 1:26–27, it can also carry a collective sense and refer to humankind in general, in which case it may be translated as *man* or *mankind*. The word *anthropos* (ἄνθρωπος) was the Greek term usually used to translate this Hebrew word, and it likewise was used both as a generic term and of individuals, from Homer downward, with the generic use usually given as the first definition by both classical and biblical lexicons. Unfortunately for the English-language reader of the NRSV, this collective definition is obliterated in these first occurrences of the word, *adam* (without the article in 26 and with it in 27) being translated *humankind* in both verses. Because of the clarification at the close of Genesis 1:27, "in the image of God he created them (but footnoted that the Hebrew reads *him*), male and female he created them," there can be no doubt as to the generic meaning of the word *man* or that of the pronoun *him* in the first clause. Only deliberate obtuseness would confuse these definitions of both words.

Nor is this ignoring of the singular *man* and *him* in Genesis 1:27 without its sad consequence. Instead of a ringing announcement of the solidarity of the human species, the reader is presented with a limitless number of individual human beings, *humankind* equaling *them* as it were. Certainly, the Hebrew text requires the numerically prohibited identification of the final *them* with the earlier *him*, a grammatical nightmare. Nevertheless, when the original is translated literally, as it was in every Authorized Version prior to the NRSV, a theologically critical statement is made about the generic nature of humanity. The presentation of the singularity of the human species generates a fundamental concept for the development of a biblically-based ethics. Sadly, current preoccupation with issues of gender-neutral language has eliminated this idea from one of its classical scriptural locations.

Genesis 1:26a–27

NRSV	RSV
Then God said, "Let us make humankind[a] in our image . . ." So God created humankind[a] in his image, in the image of God he created them;[b] male and female he created them.	Then God said, "Let us make man in our image . . ." So God created man in his own image, in the image of God he created him; male and female he created them.
NKJV	KJV
Then God said, "Let Us make man in Our image . . ." So God created man in His *own* image; in the image of God He created him; male and female He created them.	And God said, "Let us make man in our image . . ." So God created man in his *own* image, in the image of God created he him; male and female created he them.
NLT	NIV
Then God said, "Let us make people in our image . . ." So God created people . . .	The God said, "Let us make man in our image . . ." So God created man . . .
CEV	GNB
God said, "Now we will make humans . . ." So God created humans to be like himself.	Then God said, "And now we will make human beings . . ." So God created human beings, making them to be like himself.

[a]Heb *adam* [b]Heb *him*

The reader meets this translation issue, then, almost immediately upon opening the Bible when reaching the creation of humankind on Day Six. In the first two chapters of Genesis, furthermore, Creation is described twice, with the creation of humankind presented as the high point in both versions. One of these accounts is found in Genesis 1:1—2:4a and the other in Genesis 2:4b–25. The problem of gender-inclusive language must be addressed in each creation account.[1]

In both accounts, the word now often translated *humankind* is *ha-adam* (האדם) in Hebrew, where *ha* (ה) is the definite article *the*. Occasionally the Hebrew *adam* (אדם) as a personal name appears. Older versions almost always translated these terms as either *man* or *Adam*, making a judgment about whether the person is meant or the more general reference is indicated. In more contemporary versions, the term is variously translated as *man, the man, humankind,* or *Adam*. The issue, of course, is what to do with a term which is both a personal name and one which means *man*, whether used in the singular as a reference to a single man or collectively to humankind in general.

The first translation of the Old Testament, that into Greek and known as the Septuagint (abbreviated LXX), had to meet the challenge of how to manage this word. The LXX starts to talk about Adam at verse 2:16, a practice not followed by any of our English versions under consideration. Furthermore, where our contemporary versions use *the man* in verse 20, the LXX is not so particular, saying that Adam named the animals as they appeared before him. Also, in verse 23, the LXX has Adam declare that the woman was taken from *andros* (ἀνδρός, the genitive case of *aner* = ἀνήρ = *man*). By so doing, the LXX avoids the word *anthropos* (ἄθρωπος), previously used in verse 1:26 where God *created man*.

By using a different word for *man*, the Greek thereby matches the Hebrew in 2:23, which also uses a different word for *man, ish* (איש), instead of *adam*. At the same time, the Greek term for *woman, guné* (γυνή), has absolutely no relationship, alliterative or otherwise, to the Greek term used for *man (aner* and its various case forms). The translators of the **LXX** were simply unable to approximate the Hebrew *ishshah*

---

1. The first account, Genesis 1:1—2:4a, is assigned to the Priestly Source (P) and the second, Genesis 2:4b–25, to the Yahwist Source (J). As the current study is not concerned with so-called source criticism, the interested reader is referred to Campbell and O'Brien, *Sources of the Pentateuch* (1993).

(אשה) in its alliterative and possible etymological relationships to *ish* (איש).[2]

Genesis 2:7, 23b, 24a, 25a

NRSV	RSV
Then the Lord God formed man from the dust of the ground[c] . . . "this one shall be called Woman,[d] for out of Man[e] this one was taken." Therefore a man[a] leaves his father . . . And the man[a] and his wife . . .	Then the Lord God formed man of dust from the ground . . . "she shall be called Woman,[d] because she was taken out of Man."[e] Therefore a man leaves his father . . . And the man and his wife . . .
NKJV	KJV
And the Lord God formed man of the dust of the ground . . . "She shall be called Woman, because she was taken out of Man." Therefore a man shall leave his father . . . And they were both naked, the man and his wife . . .	And the Lord God formed man *of* the dust of the ground . . . "she shall be called Woman, because she was taken out of man." Therefore shall a man leave his father . . . And they were both naked, the man and his wife . . .
NLT	NIV
And the Lord God formed a man's body . . . "she was taken out of man." This explains why a man leaves his father . . . Now, although Adam and his wife . . .	—the Lord God formed the man from the dust of . . . "for she was taken out of man." For this reason a man will leave . . . The man and his wife . . .
CEV	GNB
The Lord God took a handful of soil and made a man. . . . "She came from me, a man. So I will name her Woman!" Although the man and his wife . . .	Then the Lord God took some soil from the ground and formed a man out of it . . . "she was taken out of man." The man and the woman . . .

[a] Hebrew *adam*
[d] Hebrew *ishshah*
[e] Hebrew *ish*
[c] Or *formed a man* (Heb *adam*) *of dust from the ground* (Heb *adamah*)

I find it interesting that English, German, and Spanish have managed to approximate the Hebrew with masculine and feminine terms having obvious relationships, both etymological and alliterative, while

2. BDB, 35 and 60–61: " . . . most derive איש from [אנש] . . . On the whole, probability seems to favor root איש." 61: "אנש . . . אשה n.f. woman, wife, female."

those used in French are as disparate as the Greek. In English, Adam's companion is called *woman*, taken out of *man*. The German has *Männin*, taken *vom Manne*, while Spanish reads *Varona*, taken *del varon*. In contrast, French is unable to get beyond *la femme* and *l'homme*.

In the KJV generally, where the Hebrew is *ha-adam*, we have *man* or *the man*, and if it is *adam*, then we have *Adam* as a personal name. Thus, in 2:19–23, the Hebrew *adam* is transliterated *Adam* by KJV and NKJV, while in most cases our other versions employ *man*. In 2:25, only the New Living Translation (NLT) transliterates *adam* as *Adam*.

The creation of *ha-adam* in Genesis 2:7 provides another interesting example of alliteration, albeit without gender significance, as we read that the man was formed "from the dust of the ground" (NRSV), that is, "of *ha-adamah*" (הָאֲדָמָה). Here, although any etymological relationship is questionable, the alliteration between *adam* and *adamah* is apparent. It is also worthy of note that, in Genesis 2:19, the description of the creation of "every animal of the field and every bird of the air" (NRSV) is also *out of the ground* (*ha-adamah*). Thus one can argue a relationship of substance between the animal world and that of humans. But back to Adam.

In matters of style, with the exception of the NLT, verse 2:23 is rendered as poetry by the RSV and all subsequent versions, although this is not evident in the compressed presentation in my earlier table. The RSV renders the poem in this way :

> This at last is bone of my bones
> and flesh of my flesh;
> she shall be called Woman,
> because she was taken out of Man.

The NRSV, likewise, retains these alliterative words, *Woman* and *Man*.

The NRSV poetry, however, is somewhat tortured:

> This at last is bone of my bones
> and flesh of my flesh;
> this one shall be called Woman,
> for out of Man this one was taken.

I hope there was a heated debate about changing the feminine demonstrative pronoun *tzoth* (זֹאת) from the usually rendered *she* to *this one*. The latter may be more literally correct but in this case makes terrible poetry. It seems ironic that, as we saw in the previous chapter, the NRSV editors chose to omit the demonstrative pronoun in John 14:26, where its presence could add special theological meaning to the text, while retaining it here where its presence impedes the poetical style of the verse.

That the term *ha-adam* was understood to include humankind in general, both male and female, in places beyond these early chapters of Genesis, can be seen quite clearly in a verse like Numbers 5:6, where the RSV reads, "When a man (*ish*) or woman (*ishshah*) commits any of the sins that men (*ha-adam*) commit by breaking faith with the Lord, . . ." Here it is abundantly clear that, as in English, the Hebrew word *man* (*ha-adam*) may be used to encompass both men and women, a most problematical definition in any quest for gender-neutral language. To solve this problem, the NRSV reverts to an omission in this verse, rendering it, "When a man or woman wrongs another, breaking faith with the Lord, . . ." One would hope the NRSV editors were not trying to say that human sin resulting from breaking faith with the Lord encompasses no more than people wronging one another! Yet such an understanding is the clear implication of this attempt to render Numbers 5:6 in a gender-neutral manner. To say the least, gender-inclusive renditions should not rewrite theology.

We have already noted that, in the LXX, the Greek Old Testament, the Greek word *anthropos* is the term most closely associated with the Hebrew *ha-adam*. As used in the New Testament, in addition to its simple meaning of *man*, *anthropos* may refer to human beings in general (Matt 5:13), or to a particular class (Jn 16:21), or to human beings in contrast to animals or plants (Mk 1:17). In addition to other more general meanings, it may also be used, for instance, to refer to a husband (Matt 19:10) or to a son (Matt 10:35). Because of this, the word causes as many problems for gender-neutral proponents as does its Hebrew corollary.

The rendering of First Corinthians 15:21 provides an example of how the NRSV and other inclusive versions have chosen to address the problem posed by *anthropos*. Inasmuch as we will be examining how the quest for inclusive language affects the hymns of the church, Handel's treatment of this verse from First Corinthians in his great oratorio *Messiah* is instructive. Chorus 46 is one of his most thrilling choruses, having the following libretto:

> Since by man came death, since by man came death,
> by man came also the resurrection of the dead,
> by man came also the resurrection of the dead,
> by man came also the resurrection of the dead.

This is followed by the words of verse 22:

> For as in Adam all die, for as in Adam all die,
> even so in Christ shall all be made alive,
> even so in Christ shall all be made alive,
> even so in Christ shall all,
> so in Christ shall all be made alive,
> ev'n so in Christ shall all, shall all be made alive.

I Corinthians 15:21

NRSV	RSV
For since death came through a human being, the resurrection of the dead has also come through a human being.	For as by a man came death, by a man has come also the resurrection of the dead.
NKJV	KJV
For since by man *came* death, by Man also *came* the resurrection of the dead.	For since by man *came* death, by man *came* also the resurrection of the dead.
NLT	NIV
So you see, just as death came into the world through a man, Adam, now the resurrection from the dead has begun through another man, Christ.	For since death came through a man, the resurrection of the dead comes also through a man.
CEV	GNB
Just as we will die because of Adam, we will be raised to life because of Christ.	For just as death came by means of a man, in the same way the rising from death comes by means of a man.

When a comparison is made between the more gender-neutral renderings and the classical translation of this verse rendered in music by Handel, one can only be thankful that he had before him the King James Version. He was able to quote it *verbatim*; to have done the same with any of our more modern versions would have made a hash of the entire chorus! It beggars the imagination to think of creating a libretto from "the resurrection of the dead has also come through a human being," which has neither meter nor cadence.

Nor does the concern for gender neutrality affect style alone. In a telling passage from Paul's letter to the Galatians, chapter 3:7 & 9, the

NRSV distorts the meaning of the letter while the RSV suggests that *anthropos* appears when it does not, producing one of those interesting situations where the KJV seems to contain the most satisfactory translation. The NRSV turns the Greek pronoun plus noun *those [who are] of faith* (*hoi ek pisteos*) into a verb by rendering it as *those who believe*, implying that those who believe are Abraham's descendants. Such a rendition achieves the goal of gender neutrality, but at the expense of ignoring the heavy freight that the noun *faith* (*pistis*) carries in the Galatian letter. In the time-line laid out already to the Galatians by Paul, the Christian's faith is preceded by three other aspects of faith. In the first place, God is faithful to the promise made to Abraham, having removed the curse of the law and *reckoning righteousness by faith*. Secondly, Abraham's faith is seen as the archetype of faith and the basis for the promise of salvation. Finally, the faith of Christ whereby he bore the curse of the law makes possible the salvation of the believer. The phrase *Those [who are] of faith*, then, in verses seven and nine, is thus a shorthand expression for those whom God justified on the basis of the faithfulness of Christ and in response to the promise of Abraham.

Galatians 3:7 & 9

NRSV	RSV
... so, you see, those who believe are the descendants of Abraham. ... For this reason, those who believe are blessed with Abraham who believed.	So you see that it is men of faith who are the sons of Abraham. ... So then, those who are men of faith are blessed with Abraham who had faith.
NKJV	KJV
... only those who are of faith ... those who are of faith ...	... they which are of faith ... they which are of faith ...
NLT	NIV
... those who put their faith in God ... all who put their faith in Christ ...	... those who believe ... So those who have faith ...
CEV	GNB
... everyone who has faith ... everyone who has faith ...	... the people who have faith ... all who believe ...

The NRSV, in its attempt to be gender inclusive, manages to miss all of these subtleties associated with Paul's use of the word *faith*. At the same time, the RSV does a masterful job of capturing this aspect of Paul's thought, but at the price of injecting the idea that Paul used the word *men* (*anthropoi*) when he did not. Remarkably, both the KJV and the NKJV present gender-neutral renderings that capture Paul's emphasis on the word *faith*. One must wonder why the newest Authorized Version found it impossible to copy the reading of the first, especially as that first was itself gender neutral.

The propensity for Hebrew, Aramaic, Greek, and English, the languages at issue for us, to use the word *man* to include all humankind raises general problems for those concerned about gender inclusiveness. Editors need to take great care to retain the meaning of the original while removing gender references insofar as possible. In those cases where the meaning of the masculine singular is clearly inclusive of people at large, regardless of gender, then to change it would seem to be an unwarranted attempt to rewrite Scripture in the service of re-defining the language itself. As we turn to the next chapter, we will see how the solutions implemented to resolve this issue can cause problems in another use of the word *man*.

4

The Son of Man

IN THE GOSPELS, JESUS often refers to himself as *the son of man,* a phrase that also appears in the Old Testament. We should not complete our examination of the word *man* without looking at how this phrase has fared, and we take our start with Psalm 8, where occurs one of the better known appearances of this expression:

Psalm 8:4

NRSV	RSV
What are human beings that you are mindful of them, mortals[a] that you care for them?	What is man that thou art mindful of him, and the son of man that thou dost care for him?
NKJV	KJV
What is man that You are mindful of him, and the son of man that You visit him?	What is man, that thou are mindful of him? And the son of man, that thou visitest him?
NLT	NIV
. . . what are mortals that you should think of us, mere humans that you should care for us?	. . . what is man that you are mindful of him, and the son of man that you care for him?
CEV	GNB
Then I ask, "Why do you care about us humans? Why are you concerned for us weaklings?"	. . . what is man, that you think of him; mere man, that you care for him?

[a] Heb *ben adam,* lit. *son of man*

In the NRSV, we find *human beings* and *mortals* instead of *man* and *the son of man* to translate *enosh* (אנוש = *man, mankind*) and *ben adam* (בן־אדם = *son of man*). Thus the general has been substituted for the specific, the plural for the singular. This type of substitution appears often in the Psalms, as we shall see in the next chapter. Here in Psalm 8, then, instead of finding a ringing declaration of the love and concern of God for each person individually, with all the comfort and affirmation such a recognition would convey, we find in its place a general statement about humankind at large, about the race as a whole. What has historically made the Psalms so meaningful to individual believers has been dissipated in the sea of generality.

Not only has the personal disappeared, but also the possible Messianic interpretations of this Old Testament passage have been eliminated in the pursuit of genderless language. When this portion of Psalm 8 is quoted by the NRSV in Hebrews 2:6, the changes render its application to Jesus virtually unrecognizable. Yet it is evident that, for the author of Hebrews, the Psalm makes a clear reference to Jesus, and the phrase *son of man* applies to him. In fact, by verse 9, the author of Hebrews names Jesus and sees in the words of the Psalm a description of exactly what happened to Jesus.

Hebrews 2:6–7

NRSV	RSV
But someone has testified somewhere, "What are human beings that you are mindful of them,[a] or mortals, that you care for them?[b] You have made them for a little while lower[c] than the angels; you have crowned them with glory and honor."[d]	It has been testified somewhere, "What is man that thou art mindful of him, or the son of man, that thou carest for him? Thou didst make him for a little while lower than the angels, thou hast crowned him with glory and honor."[e]
NKJV	KJV
... saying: "What is man that You ... or the son of man that You ... ? You have made him ... You have crowned him ... And set him over the works of Your hands."	... saying, What is man ... Or the son of man ... Thou madest him ... thou crownedst him ... and didst set him over the works of thy hands."
NLT	NIV
For somewhere in the Scriptures it says, "What is man ... and the son of man ... For a little while you made him ... and you crowned him ..."	But there is a place ... What is man ... the son of man ... You made him ... and crowned him with ..."
CEV	GNB
... someone says to God, "... care about us humans? ... weaklings such as us? You made us lower ... have crowned us with ..."[g]	Instead, ... Scriptures: "What is man, ... ; mere man, ... ? You made him ... You crowned him with ...[f]

[a]Gk *What is man that you are mindful of him?*

ᵇGk *or the son of man that you care for him?*
In the Hebrew of Psalm 8:4–6 both *man* and *son of man* refer to all humankind
ᶜOr *them only a little lower*
ᵈOther ancient authorities add *and set them over the works of your hands*
ᵉOther ancient authorities insert *and didst set him over the works of thy hands*
ᶠ*Many manuscripts add:* You made him ruler over everything you made (*see Ps 8:6*)
ᵍSome manuscripts add "and you have placed us in charge of all you created."

This is seen as clearly in the NRSV rendition of Hebrews 2:9 as in other versions:

> . . . but we do see Jesus, who for a little while was made lower than the angels, now crowned with glory and honor because of the suffering of death, so that by the grace of God he might taste death for everyone.

We are consequently invited to think that the author of Hebrews makes this identification between the Psalm and Jesus purely on the basis of the parallelism between his suffering and the Psalmist's vision of humankind being made lower than the angels for a little while. That this connection should be made on the basis of the *son of man* language of the Psalm itself will only become apparent to the reader of the NRSV notes, a matter itself that needs comment.

Of all the versions, it is the NRSV which has most carefully supplied notes to tell the reader what the original Greek or Hebrew actually says, and the editors deserve our praise for taking such care. But in our day and age, who reads the notes anymore? Only the most studious will spend time with the NRSV notes, while the many will claim great adherence to the Bible and to its words from the Lord, all the time missing some of the most meaningful terms because they are found only in the notes.

In similar fashion, the NRSV is the text read in worship every Sunday at most mainline churches. When the texts for the day are read, obviously the notes are never quoted, so whatever value they contribute is lost on those in the congregation. Thus, in this case, should Psalm 8 and Hebrews 2 ever occur together, the connection those hearing would make between the two would be far looser than that demanded by the New Testament text.

Psalm 144:3 is almost the same statement as that found in Psalm 8:4, yet the NRSV has no note to indicate this, not even one to refer to the earlier Psalm. In the same manner, the appearances of the *son of man* phrase in Psalms 80:17 and 146:3 are allowed to pass without comment. In fact, Psalm 80:17 manages to eschew the usual word *mortal* for its translation altogether:

> But let your hand be upon the one at your right hand, the one whom you made strong for yourself.

The careful reader would have no idea that the second half of that verse read in the RSV,

> the son of man whom thou hast made strong for thyself!

Because it omits the expected notes everywhere after Psalm 8, the reader of the NRSV will find it impossible to discuss the meaning of the phrase *the son of man* in the Psalms.

But the problem caused by the elimination of the *son of man* phrase is even more pronounced in the famous vision in the Old Testament apocalypse, Daniel, as seen in Daniel 7:13–14, where one like the son of man is envisioned coming to the Ancient of Days. The NRSV presents the reader with *one like a human being* making the approach, although once again we must be grateful for the notes which give the actual words.

Daniel 7:13–14

NRSV	RSV
I saw one like a human being[a] coming with the clouds of heaven. And he came to the Ancient One[b] and was presented before him. To him was given dominion and glory and kingship, that all peoples, nations, and languages should serve him. His dominion is an everlasting dominion that shall not pass away, and his kingship is one that shall never be destroyed.	I saw in the night visions, and behold, with the clouds of heaven there came one like a son of man, and he came to the Ancient of Days and was presented before him. And to him was given dominion and glory and kingdom, that all peoples, nations, and languages should serve him; his dominion is an everlasting dominion, which shall not pass away, and his kingdom one that shall not be destroyed.
NKJV	KJV
... One like the Son of Man ...	... one like the Son of man ...
NLT	NIV
... someone who looked like a man ...	... one like a son of man ....
CEV	GNB
what looked like a son of man[c] coming ...	... what looked like a human being. He ...

[a] Aram *one like a son of man*
[b] Aram *the Ancient of Days*

^c *son of man*: Or "human." In Aramaic "son of man" may mean a human or even "oneself" ("I" or "me"). Jesus often used the phrase "the Son of Man" when referring to himself.

What has been lost becomes immediately evident when the NRSV translation of Daniel is compared with the text we find in the Synoptic Gospels. For instance, in Matthew 25:31, as seen below, the *son of man* phrase has been retained in the NRSV, but its possible Old Testament Messianic reference in Daniel has been obliterated, as we have seen, to the confusion of both believer and aspiring student who may wonder why debates about the Gospel meaning of the phrase generated so much controversy among New Testament scholars during the twentieth century.

Matthew 25:31

NRSV	RSV
"When the Son of Man comes in his glory, and all the angels with him, then he will sit on the throne of his glory."	"When the Son of man comes in his glory, and all the angels with him, then he will sit on his glorious throne."
NKJV	KJV
"When the son of man comes in His glory"	"When the Son of man shall come in his glory"
NLT	NIV
"But when the Son of Man comes in his glory"	"When the Son of Man comes in His glory"
CEV	GNB
"When the Son of Man comes in his glory"	"When the Son of Man comes as King"

In the New Testament, the phrase occurs almost exclusively in the Gospels: fourteen times in Mark, eight in Q (material common to Matthew and Luke), eight in Matthew alone, seven in Luke alone, and thirteen times in John. Outside of the Gospels, it appears only in Revelation 1:13 and 14:14 where Daniel is the clear reference, and in Acts 7:56 recounting Stephen's vision of *the Son of Man standing at the right hand of God*. The Gospel expression is used only in sayings of Jesus, where the accompanying expansions often clarify its meaning by saying *I* or *me*. In the Synoptic Gospels, he is never addressed by this title nor does it ever appear in the narrative. That Jesus actually used it to refer to himself is generally accepted. The debate, of course, revolves around the attempt to identify what Jesus meant by using this phrase.

By the time of the Gospel of John, the meaning of the phrase is clear. In its first appearance, angels ascend and descend on the Son of Man (1:51), while in two places, the Son of Man is described as descending from heaven and ascending there again (3:13 and 6:62). In five places in John, the Son of Man is either *exalted* (3:14, 8:28, 12:34c) or *glorified* (12:23, 13:31f), and the hour of exaltation and glorification is that of the *ascent*, while in 5:27, the Son has power to sit in judgment because he is the *Son of Man*. The Daniel text clearly provides the background for the meaning of nine of the thirteen appearances of this phrase in the Gospel of John. In this respect, the use of the phrase parallels that of its use in many places in the Synoptics, although the author of John also introduces his own unique perspective Unfortunately, the reader of the NRSV will be hard put to recognize the Daniel passage in any of this because of the way the Old Testament is translated.

Ezekiel is the biblical book in which the phrase most often appears, being used almost one hundred times. The NRSV reader would hardly know that, however, as this is a place where the notes fail. At its first appearance, in 2:1,

> He said to me, "O mortal, stand up on your feet,"

the NRSV includes the following note,

> Or *son of man*; Heb *ben adam* (and so throughout the book when Ezekiel is addressed).

This is a helpful note, but is the only reference in the book or in its notes to the use of this phrase. Following this first use of the phrase, it appears in all but four chapters, being omitted only in chapters 41–42 and 45–46, where measurements and sacrificial offerings are the primary concerns. Ordinarily, the reader of Ezekiel would therefore be saturated with the *son of man* phrase, understanding it to mean simply *man*, or *fellow*, or any of the possible synonyms one could use to refer to another when in conversation. Because of its lack of notation, the reader of the NRSV will not be so sated.

That, at a minimum, Jesus was most often using the phrase in this way should be self-evident.[1] The extent to which he may have intended

---

1. For a detailed and challenging look at the evidence for this, see Wink, *The Human*

more than this remains the subject of debate, although there is no doubt that the New Testament writers understood the phrase to include the model from Daniel as well. As participants in the debate, readers of the NRSV can be thankful that *son of man* has been faithfully translated in its New Testament appearances, but must regret that its Old Testament background has been obscured in the cause of gender neutrality, thereby limiting the utility of this version as a study Bible.

Being: Jesus and the Enigma of the Son of Man (2002), although many will find unwarranted the conclusion he draws from his examination.

5

Impersonality in Psalms and Proverbs

THE EFFECT OF THIS emphasis on gender-neutral language in the translation of the books of Psalms and Proverbs is particularly marked and unfortunate. As we noted in the preceding chapter when discussing Psalm 8, much of the appeal in these books comes from the intensely personal expressions found in them, feelings with which the individual believer can readily identify. Because of the *androcentric* nature of the Bible in general and the highly emotional situations often encountered in the language of the Psalms in particular, readers have regularly identified with the psalmist and have made the Psalms perhaps the favorite biblical book. Sad to say, almost all of these personal references have disappeared in the books of Psalms and Proverbs as they are found in the NRSV.

For instance, consider the beginning of the Book of Psalms. In the very first Psalm, the singular man is set in opposition to the many ungodly around him, but when the man is made to disappear into a group of genderless people, then a part of the meaning of the passage is lost. No longer is an individual tempted by the advice of the ungodly; neither is the source of a single person's happiness raised as an issue for contemplation. Furthermore, that such a person can be rooted and grounded by devotion to the Lord, no matter what may be happening round about, is lost in the generality of the plural as this Psalm is now presented.

Psalm 1:1–3

NRSV	RSV
Happy are those who do not follow the advice of the wicked, or take the path that sinners tread, or sit in the seat of scoffers; but their delight is in the law of the Lord, and on his law they meditate day and night. They are like trees planted by streams of water . . .	Blessed is the man[a] who walks not in the counsel of the wicked, nor stands in the way of sinners, nor sits in the seat of scoffers; but his delight is in the law of the Lord, and on his law he meditates day and night. He is like a tree planted by streams of water . . .
NKJV	**KJV**
Blessed is the man . . . but his delight . . . He shall be like a tree . . .	Blessed is the man . . . But his delight . . . And he shall be like a tree . . .
NLT	**NIV**
Oh, the joys of those . . . But they delight . . . They are like trees . . .	Blessed is the man . . . But his delight . . . He is like a tree . . .
CEV	**GNB**
God blesses those people . . . the Law of the Lord makes them happy . . . They are like trees . . .	Happy are those . . . Instead, they find joy . . . They are like trees . . .

[a] Hebrew איש = *ish*, which can only mean "man" as distinguished from woman.

It is inviting to identify oneself with an individual in a text; it is more difficult to perceive the possibility of such an identification when one is reading about a group rather than an individual. When the text under discussion is an Old Testament Psalm, the loss of this invitation is more than a simply deficient literary device. It is, rather, a spiritual disservice to the believer. One might even argue that, instead of augmenting an experience with God's Word, this change from the singular to the plural form in the NRSV serves to separate a reader from the Word of God. That the following shows such a change to have been unnecessary makes it doubly tragic:

> Happy is the one who does not follow the advice of the wicked, or take the path that sinners tread, . . . but delights in the law of the Lord, etc.

Such a rendering would have preserved the personal nature of the Psalm and rendered it gender neutral, as well. One can surely wonder why at points like these the translators chose to ignore the critical link between personal language and correlated theological issues.

Similar reservations seem to be called for in about twenty other places (5:5, 25:12, 32:2, etc.). Elsewhere, the gender-neutral NRSV renderings seem to raise no such issues. One can see this in places like Psalm 12:1,

> ... the faithful have disappeared from humankind,"

where the plural *sons of men* is neutralized by the use of *humankind*, or Psalm 18:25, where *man* is simply a general singular and can actually be omitted in favor of its modifying adjective standing alone (i.e., *blameless*, instead of *blameless man*). In these, as in many other verses, rendering the singular masculine with its modifier alone or with a plural form makes no difference. The personal relationship between the Divine and the believer is not at issue and there is no implied invitation to the reader or singer to identify with the psalmist.

Furthermore, the use of some plurals in combination with singular words is becoming increasingly acceptable in English. For instance, in spoken English, few people today would complete a sentence like "No one brought _____ book to class" with any pronoun other than "their," to the dismay of grammarians, who know that grammar is taught not to persecute students but to provide the tools for clarity of thought and expression. So it is that, in the NRSV rendition of many of the Psalms, the substitution of the plural for the singular *man*, *he*, or *him* has little effect on the meaning of the verse for the contemporary reader.

I find it interesting, however, that in places the NRSV has retained the word *man* in spite of the specific editorial directions to the contrary detailed earlier in the Introduction:

> ... in references to men and women, masculine-oriented language should be eliminated as far as this can be done without altering passages that reflect the historical situation of ancient patriarchal culture.[1]

For instance, the NRSV renders Psalm 19:4b–5, as follows,

> In the heavens he has set a tent for the sun, which comes out like a bridegroom from his wedding canopy, and like a strong man runs its course with joy.

---

1. *New Revised Standard Version*, viii.

Other versions talk about an athlete running, and even the NIV, not known for its concern for gender-neutral language, talks about a *champion* running. Similar exceptions in the NRSV occur in Psalms 127 and 128, where we find

> Happy is the man who has his quiver full of them. (i.e., *sons*)

in 127:5, and

> Thus shall the man be blessed who fears the Lord.

in 128:4. Can this last not also be said of a woman, and if so, how has this *man* escaped the NRSV editor's notice?

At the same time, in those verses of Psalm 109 where the psalmist is praying for curses to come upon his accuser, no attempt is made to eliminate either the noun *man* or the masculine singular third person pronoun. Psalm 109:6–7 is rendered,

> They say, "Appoint a wicked man against him; let an accuser stand on his right. When he is tried, let him be found guilty; let his prayer be counted as sin."

For the next twelve verses, maledictions are declared against *him* and *his* without embarrassment over the gender-specific nature of the language. Apparently it is acceptable for the masculine singular to be used to describe malefactors but not the righteous. This does not seem to be an attempt to create a gender-level playing field, but rather one to tilt the field from patriarchal forms to an anti-masculine bias. If such is the case, it has no place in biblical translation, which is a challenging enough enterprise without the addition of such extraneous concerns.

Where the retention of the singular does make a difference, however, I wish the use of pronouns in the first or second person had been generally followed, as adopted, for instance, by the NRSV in Psalm 37:23–24,

> Our steps are made firm by the Lord, when he delights in our way; though we stumble, we shall not fall headlong, for the Lord holds us by the hand.

In these verses, *Our steps* appears instead of *A man's steps*, *our way* replaces *his way*, and so forth. The thought concludes with the assertion that we are held in the Lord's hand, a sentiment that cannot be expressed in language any more personal. I think it unfortunate that, since the decision had already been made not to translate the masculine third person singular, the NRSV editors ignored the possibilities afforded by the first and second person, notably where the personal element is so commanding. No gender is associated with *I, me,* or *you,* this last serving for both singular and plural with the disappearance of *thou* from general use. They could have served well as substitutes for *he* and *him* in many places where the personal is at issue.

On the other hand, the NRSV's use of the first person in Psalm 94:11, where it refers to fools and the dullest of people, while using plurals to translate *man* and masculine pronouns elsewhere, is unfortunate. The NRSV then proceeds in the following verse to say, *Happy are those . . . ,* thereby moving to the plural when referring to persons with whom the Lord is dealing positively. Something certainly seems to be wrong here.

Psalm 94:11

NRSV	RSV
The Lord knows our thoughts,[a] that they are but an empty breath.	The Lord knows the thoughts of man, that they are but a breath.
NKJV	KJV
The Lord knows the thoughts of man, that they are futile.	The Lord knoweth the thoughts of man, that they are vanity.
NLT	NIV
The Lord knows people's thoughts, that they are worthless.	The Lord knows the thoughts of man; he knows that they are futile.
CEV	GNB
The Lord knows how useless our plans really are.	The Lord knows what they think; he knows how senseless their reasoning is.

[a]Heb *the thoughts of humankind*

As a side note, the same can be said about some of the renderings in Proverbs, where this same result can be seen in renderings like that of Proverbs 16:9:

The human mind plans the way, . . .

Somehow, the phrase *the human mind* lacks the cachet of *a man's mind,* just as it lacks the direct appeal found in the latter phrase. This is the situation in a half-dozen places in Proverbs (3:13, 5:21, 15:18, etc.).

50 THE SEDUCTION OF THE CHURCH

Proverbs 16:9

NRSV	RSV
The human mind plans the way, but the Lord directs the steps.	A man's mind plans his way, but the Lord directs his steps.
NKJV	**KJV**
A man's heart . . .	A man's heart . . .
NLT	**NIV**
We can make our plans, but the Lord determines our steps.	In his heart a man plans his course . . .
CEV	**GNB**
We make our own plans, but the Lord decides where we will go.	You make your plans, but the Lord directs your actions.

In this case, again the singular is eschewed, although a collective construction is used rather than a plural. Even so, the invitation for an individual reader to identify with this planner and his divinely directed steps is muted by the phraseology employed. In contrast, both the CEV and the GNB demonstrate how the use of either the first or second person pronoun would retain this possibility for individual identification.

In the one case, that of the *we* whose destination is decided by the Lord, the individual reader would seem to have the choice of identifying with *the rest of us* or not, depending on the person's predilections. In the other, since the second person pronoun *you* may refer to either a group or an individual, no choice would appear available. It is simple for the reader to apply these words directly to herself or himself. I choose not to say *themselves* in this situation because of the point I am hoping to make, although it would be possible given the vagaries of contemporary spoken English.

As in the Psalms, however, a host of places are found in Proverbs where the move to gender-neutral language seems to have been made without causing any problems. In Proverbs 3:30, for instance, the admonition,

> Do not quarrel with anyone without cause,

would actually seem to capture the sense of the original. Anyone reading,

> Do not quarrel with a man etc.

would hardly understand it to approve of a causeless quarrel with a woman! In this case, the NRSV reading has created an improvement of the text. Although this may not be said about every one of these changes, that it does apply to some deserves mention.

Proverbs as rendered by the NRSV also preserves one chapter where *man* and the masculine singular pronouns *he* and *him* are found. Chapter seven is devoted to the encouragement of a chaste life, doing so with many verses depicting a prostitute's seduction of *a young man without sense*, so described in 7:7. For the following sixteen verses, *he* and *his* ensnarement by the wiles of the *wicked lady* are recounted. Upon reaching the final four verses of the chapter, when attention is turned to the moral of the story, it is addressed to *my children* in 7:24 instead of *O sons*. In Proverbs, as in Psalms, apparently it is suitable to continue the use of the masculine if stupidity, venality, or wickedness is being described, but not otherwise. I suppose many feminist authors and comedians would suggest that such use sounds pretty normal. In the translation of Scripture, however, it is highly questionable. I am reminded of the comment by Liz Curtis Higgs:

> Funny: The older scholars blamed the women for everything and painted the men as heroes. The newer writers blamed the men for everything and described the women as victims and the men as jerks. The truth lies somewhere in the middle, so that's what I aimed for: balance. And truth.[2]

I hope to find both balance and truth in this study, as well.

The quest for the use of gender-inclusive language in Scripture has led to the unfortunate elimination in the NRSV of much of the personal element that has made the Old Testament Psalms so meaningful to believers through the years. Whether Psalms will consequently retain its historic place as the most popular book in the Bible remains to be seen. What makes this situation so sad is the realization that both Psalms and Proverbs could have been rendered in ways that, while preserving their highly personal rhetoric, were at the same time gender neutral. And not only is it sad that this was not done, but it is also unconscionable to have committed such an atrocity upon the newest Authorized Version of the Bible, namely, the New Revised Standard Version.

---

2. Higgs, *Bad Girls*, 6.

As I have already discussed at the conclusion of chapter two, the NRSV is the pew Bible in mainline Protestant churches. This elimination of the personal element in both Psalms and Proverbs means that one of the most important scriptural expressions of the individual relationship possible between the believer and the Divine has disappeared. The public reading of these portions of Scripture in worship, and even the study of them now in classes, will hardly evoke the intensity of response heretofore expected when Psalms and Proverbs were the topics of discussion.

Furthermore, the combination of this catastrophe with the disappearance of personal language for use in talking about God is disastrous. Although the NRSV in general continues to use personal language in its talk about God, as we have noted several times, the same cannot be said about the leadership of our churches, which seems unable to emulate the language of Scripture. For the most part, the church has now been led for a generation by clergy and others who refuse to use the personal language in their vocabulary to talk about God, thereby depriving believers in their care of essential terms for a vibrant faith.

In these circles, "God talk" of a personal nature has been almost entirely restricted to the first and second person, to *I*, *we*, and *you*. These pronouns are meaningful when the subject of discussion involves the speaker's individual piety, a piety that hearers may be invited to emulate. The object of such piety, however, must be described in the third person, and herein lies the rub, as our leaders now eschew the use of the natural language about God as found in the NRSV. When they do talk about the acts or the words or the nature of God, it is in a language so contrived that any native speaker of English recognizes something as phony, even when what it is may be unclear.

The consequences of such impersonality both in the language of these important portions of the Bible and in the liturgy of the church would appear to be dire. Although the mainline Protestant churches tend no longer to use phrases like "personal relationship with the Lord" to describe the believer's position before the Almighty, they have nevertheless always insisted that God is a personal Being, a spiritual Being with whom a believer can relate in a personal way. With the disappearance of personal language for use in talking about God, the worshiping believer is suddenly faced with the impossible task of being invited to think about God in personal terms but without the language to do so. Is there any wonder that confusion reigns in the pew?

6

O Brother, Who Art Thou?

No word signals the patriarchal nature of the Bible more than the word *brother*. Although it obviously means the male children of the same parents, in the languages of Scripture it has broader meanings as well, and this in both the singular and plural. Consequently, the term poses peculiar problems for the translator, since in English the singular is almost always gender specific, although the plural often has a broader connotation much like that found in the original biblical languages.

We first meet the term with the story of Cain and Abel in the fourth chapter of the book of Genesis, immediately after the expulsion of the first couple from the Garden of Eden. Cain, who became a farmer, a *tiller of the ground*, is born first. His birth is followed in short order by that *of his brother Abel*, who became a shepherd. As the story of the first sacrifice unfolds, both brothers take offerings from their work, Abel *of the firstlings of his flock, their fat portions*, and Cain *of the fruit of the ground*. Then, as told in the NRSV, "And the Lord had regard for Abel and his offering, but for Cain and his offering he had no regard." Shortly thereafter, the angry Cain kills Abel.

What follows is one of the most famous and meaningful dialogues in Scripture. The Lord accosts Cain with the question, *Where is Abel your brother?* Like the question in the preceding chapter of Genesis, where the Lord is seeking the hidden Adam and Eve and calling, *Where are you?*, this question to Cain is not seeking information. Instead, the object of the question is to elicit a confession of guilt, an admission Cain has no intention of making. Unlike Adam, Cain answers with a defiant repudiation of responsibility.

After pleading ignorance, Cain adds what is clearly a rhetorical question, *Am I my brother's keeper?* The story moves on immediately to the Lord's denunciation of Cain for what he has done, with the gripping claim that the blood of Abel cries out from the ground itself, of which Cain himself is the *tiller*. Although the story moves on, however, the moral principle raised by Cain's question, with its plainly implied answer of *Yes!*, is one that any ethical system must address. To the extent that this is the case, it is equally clear that the word *brother*, which in this case refers to Abel, the specific brother at issue, applies also to humankind in general. And it is this broader application through the years that has given this story its impact. That no one can escape the realization of having hurt some other human being, even if not with a mortal stroke like Cain gave Abel, drives us all to repentance and confession.

The extension of the meaning of *brother* is not restricted to this passage in Genesis, however. For instance, it may be seen in the Old Testament text behind the second Great Commandment as identified by Jesus, namely, Leviticus 19:18b, *You shall love your neighbor as yourself.*

Leviticus 19:17-18

NRSV	RSV
You shall not hate in your heart anyone of your kin; you shall reprove your neighbor, or you will incur guilt yourself. You shall not take vengeance or bear a grudge against any of your people, but you shall love your neighbor as yourself; I am the Lord.	You shall not hate your brother in your heart, but you shall reason with your neighbor, lest you bear sin because of him. You shall not take vengeance or bear any grudge against the sons of your own people, but you shall love your neighbor as yourself: I am the Lord.
NKJV	KJV
You shall not hate your brother . . . rebuke your neighbor . . . love your neighbor as yourself . . .	Thou shalt not hate thy brother . . . rebuke thy neighbor, . . . love thy neighbor as thyself . . .
NLT	NIV
Do not nurse hatred for any of your relatives. Confront your neighbors . . . love your neighbor as yourself . . .	Do not hate your brother . . . Rebuke your neighbor . . . love your neighbor as yourself . . .
CEV	GNB
Don't hold grudges. . . . it's wrong not to correct someone who needs correcting. . . . love others as much as you love yourself . . .	Do not bear a grudge against anyone, but settle your differences with him . . . love your neighbor as you love yourself . . .

The two-verse text in Leviticus is a legal form of the moral principle elucidated in narrative form by the Cain and Abel story. And as in the story, here also the word *brother* has a broader application, being synonymous with the gender-neutral term *neighbor*. Whereas the NRSV was faithful in Genesis to retain *brother*, obviously because of the specific application to Abel, it refrains from that translation of the Hebrew (אח = *ach* = *brother*) here. Yet in these verses it is clear that the word has a broad application encompassing a host of other people, including even *the alien* if the command in verse 34 *to love the alien as yourself* is seen as a comment on verse 18. How widely this host extends is, of course, the question posed in the Gospel of Luke where this commandment is the introduction to the Parable of the Good Samaritan (Luke 10:25–37), the story told by Jesus in response to the query, *Who is my neighbor?*

As elsewhere, even though the gender-specific word is obviously not what is meant in the Leviticus passage, the NRSV has nevertheless eliminated it in favor of something gender neutral. In this case, what has been chosen is the rather insipid phrase, *any of your kin*, and this without even a note to indicate the original reading. The same may be said about the treatment of *brother* in several other places in the Old Testament, like Psalm 50:20, Proverbs 17:17, or 18:9 and 24.

The most that can be said for this phrase in Leviticus is that it is inclusive. That it carries even a hint of the solidarity of the term *brother* is something that I find hard to recognize. The application of the term *brother* to humanity in general is to clearly imply a corporate understanding of the human species that only a few other words can suggest. To refrain from using the term when its broader meaning is crystal clear is to make an unnecessary alteration in the meaning of Scripture. It seems to me that this is what the NRSV has perpetrated with its translation of these verses from Leviticus and the several additional places in the Old Testament where the broader meaning of the word is obvious.

In the New Testament, the word *brother* in the singular (ἀδελφός = *adelphos* = *brother*) almost always refers to an individual person, either someone's physical brother or a fellow follower of Jesus. Thus the NRSV shows no reluctance about translating the word literally in many of these cases. For instance, it easily translates Mark 3:35 with its parallels, *Whoever does the will of God is my brother and sister and mother*. In most places, the word is equally obvious.

There are exceptions, however, in places where the word refers to Jesus' followers. Two instances should suffice to illustrate the problem, one from Paul's writings and one from the Gospel of Luke. In Paul's first letter to the Corinthian church, he uses the word *brother* to refer to the members of the church at Corinth. The NRSV has chosen to translate the word *brother* as *believer*, but with a footnote to indicate the original. Ordinarily, one might think this a fortuitous change, making the verse gender inclusive, seemingly without any change of meaning. Unfortunately, this reading does change the understanding of the text, as it invites the reader to consider a contrast between *believer* and *unbeliever*, while Paul is concerned with disputes between one believer and another. The unbeliever only appears because believer disputants seem willing to seek settlements in the courts of non-believers. In other words, the NRSV reading dilutes some of Paul's horror at the enormity of such disputes between fellow members of the body of Christ.

I Corinthians 6:5–6

NRSV	RSV
I say this to your shame. Can it be that there is no one among you wise enough to decide between one believer[a] and another, but a believer[a] goes to court against a believer[a]—and before unbelievers at that?	I say this to your shame. Can it be that there is no man among you wise enough to decide between members of the brotherhood, but brother goes to law against brother, and that before unbelievers?
NKJV	KJV
...between his brethren? But brother ... brother ...	... between his brethren? But brother ... brother ...
NLT	NIV
...these arguments? But instead one Christian ... another ...	... believers? But instead, one brother ... another ...
CEV	GNB
... one follower and another? Why should one of you ... another ...	... fellow Christians. Instead, one Christian ... another ...

[a]Gk brother

Beyond this, the term *believer* incorporates the concept of one individual among many, laying emphasis upon the commitment of that person. In contrast, *brother* suggests a relationship between people who have something in common. Furthermore, the latter term also injects the theological topic of adoption into the discussion, with its emphasis upon the relationship of believers with Christ. Standing by itself, as it does in these verses, the term *believer* raises neither of these ideas. It can only sustain the concept of individual piety.

The Gospel illustration is less problematical. In Luke 17:3, *brother* is used to refer to Jesus' disciples, whom he is addressing directly on the topic of *occasions for stumbling* (17:1). Inasmuch as women were among the disciples who followed Jesus, it would seem perfectly appropriate that the NRSV substitute "disciple" for "brother," and we should be grateful for the note to indicate the original Greek. On the other hand, following the Leviticus model discussed earlier, one might have stressed the familial nature of the movement with words like, *if any of your kinfolk in the faith sins* . . . Kinfolk hardly equates with brother to indicate a close family relationship, but it is certainly more suitable than disciple for this purpose.

Luke 17:3

NRSV	RSV
Be on your guard! If another disciple[a] sins, you must rebuke the offender, and if there is repentance, you must forgive.	Take heed to yourselves; if your brother sins, rebuke him, and if he repents, forgive him.
NKJV	KJV
Take heed to yourselves. If your brother . . .	Take heed to yourselves: If thy brother . . .
NLT	NIV
I am warning you! If another believer sins . . .	So watch yourselves. "If your brother . . ."
CEV	GNB
So be careful what you do. Correct any followers of mine . . .	So watch what you do! If your brother . . .

[a] Gk *your brother*

This verse also gives a good picture of the way the NRSV treats the masculine singular pronouns *he*, *his*, and *him* when they are used to refer to people in general. As can be seen, the text is rearranged so they can be omitted completely. In this case, another noun is used, *offender*, although here it might have been possible to use the plural *them*, given the way the language has been changing. As a rule, however, the NRSV has been careful to avoid such grammatical inaccuracies in its use of pronouns, and has instead substituted nouns in the place of the omitted singular pronouns. As we noted earlier in chapter 5, the exception to this rule seems to have been when these pronouns refer to evil doers, when they are allowed to remain.

Incidentally, the CEV inserts this note to explain its word *followers*: "The Greek text has 'brothers,' which is often used in the New Testament for followers of Jesus." This is a surprisingly misleading statement for an American Bible Society publication. It is absolutely true that the word *brothers* is often used in the New Testament for followers of Jesus, but it is equally false to say that in this place the Greek text has the plural, *brothers*. The reading of the Greek text is the singular, *brother*, and the CEV note should have made this distinction. Be that as it may, it does move us to the NRSV treatment of the plural.

In the plural, this word was translated as *brethren* in earlier days, but now is regularly rendered as *brothers*. A problematical aspect of the word for modern translators, however, is that in Greek its plural form has extensions of meaning beyond what is possible in English. For instance, as far back as the fifth century BCE, we find the plural used to mean *brother(s) and sister(s)*. About 413 BCE, Euripides' play *Electra* was presented, in which we find the word by itself in the plural:

> ELECTRA. How could feet make any impression on a rocky surface? And if they could, the feet of brother and sister, of man and woman would not be equal, but the foot of the male is larger.[1]

Here, both setting and context require the Greek, "the feet of the *adelphown*," [genitive plural of *adelphos*] to be rendered not *brothers* but *brother and sister*. The use of the plural of *brother* with this same meaning is found elsewhere as well after this date. All of which is to say that the plural of the Greek word for *brother* poses some unique challenges to the biblical translator.

In the Gospels and Acts, the word is usually translated as *brothers* by the NRSV, although in a few places it is rendered *friends* (Acts 1:16; 6:3) or *believers*, (Acts 21:7; 28:14, 15) with a footnote to indicate the original. It even becomes *students* once (Matt. 23:8), but again with the footnote. In Paul's letters, however, the "Euripidean model" is adopted and, beginning with its first appearance in Romans 1:17, the plural word *brothers* is usually translated *brothers and sisters*. There are exceptions,

---

1. Hadas, *Euripides*, 219.

of course, where terms like *my own people* or *love one another* are used instead by the NRSV, and in the Revelation it is rendered *comrades* three times out of its four occurrences (12:10, 19:10, 22:9). Nevertheless, most of the time the plural is translated as *brothers and sisters*.

Inasmuch as English has no single word to approximate the extended meaning that is possible with *adelphoi*, the plural of the Greek word *brother*, this translation may be the most suitable available. It does, however, eliminate an important element of Paul's thought, perhaps best expressed in Galatians 3:28:

> There is no longer Jew or Greek, there is no longer slave or free, there is no longer male and female; for all of you are one in Christ Jesus. (NRSV)

His use of the final *and* seems to reveal a recognition of the ineradicable distinction of sex, with Paul arguing that even this distinction disappears *in Christ*. Having to resort to *brothers and sisters* introduces the male–female division into the "body of Christ." By being able to use a single word, especially one like *brother* with its familial nature, Paul is able both to accentuate the unity of Christian believers and to allude to their adoption as siblings in Christ. Apparently, we no longer have the English vocabulary to embrace Pauline thought in this regard.

A particularly telling example of this problem may be found in Paul's letter to the Romans, in the verses leading up to his marvelous paean in 8:38–39:

> For I am convinced that neither death, nor life, nor angels, nor rulers, nor things present, nor things to come, nor powers, nor height, nor depth, nor anything else in all creation, will be able to separate us from the love of God in Christ Jesus our Lord. (NRSV)

Paul introduces the argument leading to this conclusion by elaborating upon the providence of God who controls history and its acts, then personalizes it in 8:29.

Romans 8:29

NRSV	RSV
For those whom he foreknew he also predestined to be conformed to the image of his Son, in order that he might be the firstborn within a large family.[a]	For those whom he foreknew he also predestined to be conformed to the image of his Son, in order that he might be the first-born among many brethren.
NKJV	KJV
... He foreknew ... predestined ... among many brethren.	... did foreknow ... did predestinate ... among many brethren.
NLT	NIV
For God knew his people in advance, and he chose them to become like his Son, so that his Son would be the firstborn, with many brothers and sisters.	... God foreknew ... he predestined ... among many brothers.
CEV	GNB
and he has always known who his chosen ones would be. He had decided to let them become like his own Son, so that his Son would be the first of many children.	Those whom God had already chosen he also set apart to become like his Son, so that the Son would be the first among many brothers.

[a] Gk *among many brothers*

The adoption of the believer in Christ is clearly the theological end Paul has in mind by this allusion to predestination, but by rendering *many brethren* as *a large family* the NRSV fails to do justice to his thought. Again, one cannot fault the inclusion of a note to indicate the original, making it possible for a reader to grasp the depth of Paul's argument. It must be noted, however, that a family includes, among others, cousins, nieces and nephews, and uncles and aunts as well. The relationship Paul is stressing between Christ and believers is much closer than any of these. Even the *first of many children* rendition in the CEV comes closer to grasping Paul's thought. As the Authorized Version read aloud in public worship, this text in the NRSV fails to allow the hearer to appreciate the full extent of Paul's argument.

There are also places where the word *brothers* occurs several times within a few verses, and sometimes a different word is used for each of these appearances. An example of this is found early in Paul's letter to the Galatians, in verses 1:2, 1:11, and 2:4. In all the older versions, the translation *brothers* or *brethren* is simply repeated with each occurrence. Given its charge to eliminate masculine-specific words, however, the NRSV cannot follow this procedure, and instead chooses different words. At its first appearance, the phrase *all the members of God's family* is used instead of *all the brethren*, and the same criticism can be leveled against this reading as is made in the preceding paragraph. On the second occasion, the usual *brothers and sisters* phrase is used to translate the plural *brothers*, about which comments have already been made. Finally, *believers* is used the third time, and I would note again that this term stresses individual piety. Yet the problem being addressed by Paul in his argument here concerns the relationship of believers one to another, something implicit in the term *brothers*.

Galatians 1:2, 1:11, 2:4

NRSV	RSV
and all the members of God's family[a] who are with me . . . For I want you to know, brothers and sisters[b] . . . But because of false believers[c] secretly brought in . . .	and all the brethren who are with me . . . For I would have you know, brethren . . . But because of false brethren secretly brought in . . .
NKJV	KJV
and all the brethren who are with me . . . But I make known to you, brethren . . . and *this occurred* because of false brethren . . .	And all the brethren which are with me . . . But I certify you, brethren . . . And that because of false brethren unawares brought in . . .
NLT	NIV
All the brothers and sisters here . . . Dear brothers and sisters . . . so-called Christians there— false ones, really — . . .	and all the brothers . . . brothers . . . false brothers . . .
CEV	GNB
omits first half of verse 2 . . . My friends, . . . those who pretended to be followers . . .	All the brothers . . . my brothers, . . . Pretending to be fellow believers, . . .

[a]Gk *all the brothers*
[b]Gk *brothers*
[c]Gk *false brothers*

To reiterate this chapter's initial thesis, the words *brother* and *brothers* pose peculiar problems for translators seeking a gender-neutral version of the Bible. The choices made by the NRSV here, as in other places, successfully eliminate the gender-specificity of the terms, but create other problems, especially in terms of Pauline thought. It may be time, however, to end this examination of Scripture so we can turn our attention to the hymns of the Church.

To conclude this look at the latest Authorized Version, then, it is important to note initially that standard English usage has been retained by the NRSV in its language about God. This means that, although God is understood as a genderless spirit, the first person singular masculine pronouns are allowed to have their usual default function as the singular pronoun when person but not gender is the issue.

In contrast, the NRSV goes to extreme lengths to eliminate masculine, gender-specific nouns and pronouns elsewhere. This has created problems in particular with the treatment of the word *man* and the phrase *son of man*, especially when connections between the two Testaments are at issue. In addition, much of the personal attraction of the books of Psalms and Proverbs has been eliminated, as the singular has been replaced by the plural, thereby subsuming the individual believer into the corporate mass. Concerns about the treatment of the words *brother* and *brothers* have been the subject of this chapter. Fortunately for the reader, however, the NRSV has been careful, *most of the time*, to footnote the changes made, so it is almost always possible to identify gender-specific changes.

Let us now address the hymns of the Church.

Part Two

Gender-Neutral Language in Song

7

Beautiful Savior

Music sets the atmosphere of the church service, communicates doctrine through singing, and expresses the singers' views of what God is like. In the words of Sheldon Sorge, "A familiar hymn evokes in us a world of associations that confirm, shape and strengthen our deepest faith commitments."[1] For such reasons, music has often been a "hot potato" in the life of the church, and the subject may never have been more controversial than during the past fifty years. At one end of the spectrum are those who would say that the only words fit to be sung in the church are those of the Old Testament Psalms, and those without any musical accompaniment. At the other end are those who say that any kind of music, be it rock, pop, jazz, punk, or anything else that "turns people on," is quite legitimate for use in worship and evangelism. Somewhere in between these two extremes exist those of us still moved by the classical hymns of the faith but wrestling with issues like that of gender-neutral language.

It has been said that, "The history of hymnody is in many respects the history of the Church itself, its worship, and especially its sacred poetry."[2] This is correct—and we should therefore give its use in the life of the church serious and God-centered attention. To this end, the words of our hymns need to be measured by their reflection of biblical teachings as they have informed the church's doctrine through the years.

In his *Summa Theologiae*, Thomas Aquinas wrote, "Vocal praise of God is necessary, therefore, not for his sake but for our own, since by praising him our devotion is aroused."[3] When we sing, what we sing

1. Sorge, "Don't Mess with my Music," 15.
2. JCRH, *The Hymnal 1940 Companion*, ix.
3. Aquinas, *ST*, II–II, 91, 1c, quoted in Eco, *The Aesthetics of Thomas Aquinas*, 132.

should lift our hearts to God in adoration, petition, and self-offering. And in a very real measure, it is in the hymns of the church that the faith of believers has been distilled and most Christians express their most deeply felt convictions about God. The story is told of Karl Barth, the great twentieth-century theologian, that on one of his visits to the United States he was asked if he could summarize the essence of his theology in one statement. This great thinker, whose *Die Kirchliche Dogmatik* is a multi-volume, encyclopedia-sized work, replied, "Jesus loves me, this I know, for the Bible tells me so." Even the greatest can distill theology into singable words!

The hymns sung in congregational worship both reflect and shape the faith and actions of church members. Regardless of what other issues may be addressed, what is sung reflects the believers' deepest sense of who God is, who they are, and what God calls the church to be and to do. Our favorite hymns are those that both move our emotions and at the same time reinforce those spiritual convictions about which we feel most deeply. In a powerful way, treasured hymns open us to the sense of the Holy Spirit's near and transforming presence.

Hymns are a form of poetry, and many took form first as poems, only later being set to music. Interestingly, the editors of hymnals through the years have felt free to exercise poetic license in their effort to avoid offensive words or phrases. As the generations have passed, perceived offenses have changed but the words of those hymns so altered seldom revert to the original, as the concerns of a particular generation usually seem to become part of the succeeding general culture. One may certainly question the arrogance of these editors, so willing to change an author's words without even a note to indicate what has been done. It is as if the only words that count are those approved by the hymnal editors, without any consideration of the possibility that the author of the poem or hymn may have been even more concerned about finding the "just right" words to express exactly what she or he intended to say. It would appear that hymnal editors, especially the more recent ones, have been willing to violate an author's "voice" in a shameless way, especially in their willingness to modify historic texts.

In this regard, the concern about gender-specific language in our hymns fits within a broader movement aimed at removing supposedly artificial religious hurdles that may inhibit a meaningful connection between potential believers and God. *The Presbyterian Hymnal* expressed this concern with these words in the first paragraph of its Preface:

> The General Assembly of 1980 and 1983 directed that a hymnal be developed "using inclusive language and sensitive to the diverse nature" of the church. . . . They sought to affirm the centrality of the sacraments, ecumenical and mission dimensions, the perspectives of women, and the concerns of youth and age.[4]

This statement about gender makes clear that such issues are to constitute one of the four central affirmations of the work. As we shall see, the Presbyterians have been scrupulous in their attention to the issue of gender-inclusive language in their hymnal.

The most recent of these hymnals, the UCC's *The New Century Hymnal*, is even more specific in this regard. In its attempt to follow the directions of the 1977 General Synod XI of the UCC "to create a new official hymnal using language that is inclusive," it noted:

> In addition to this broad process of selection, every text underwent careful scrutiny of its metaphors and pronouns that refer to God, Christ, and the Spirit. Why the scrutiny? Because for nearly two millennia these words have tended toward exclusively masculine characterization, bearing painful consequences, especially for women. Every effort was made to ensure that all hymns spoke to and for all God's people, equally.[5]

The hymnal committee went on to assert that in their revisions of hymn language, they maintained "the nuance and intent of the original." In my examination of hymns in what follows, I shall invite you, the reader, to consider the accuracy of this statement.

The following chapters address various examples of the rendering of hymns into gender-inclusive language. Rather than "cherry-pick" a number of lines extracted from many different hymns, three hymns in the public domain will be examined: *Fairest Lord Jesus*; *Joyful, Joyful, We Adore Thee*; and *The God of Abraham Praise*. The chapters devoted to each of these will then be followed by one looking at the way omissions have been employed to achieve gender inclusiveness, and then another looking at what has happened with various Christmas carols in the effort to eliminate gender-specific references. The last of these chapters will

---

4. McKim, *The Presbyterian Hymnal*, 7.
5. Clyde, *The New Century Hymnal*, x.

compare an historic hymn with a newer version approved in 1974 by the Ecumenical Women's Center. Let us then turn our attention to one of the most loved of all hymns, *Fairest Lord Jesus*.

Our first hymn of special interest, *Fairest Lord Jesus*, is sung to a tune supposedly based on a twelfth-century CRUSADER HYMN.[6] A more credible suggestion is that it was sung by the followers of John Hus, who were driven out of Bohemia in 1620 in the anti-Reformation purge, settling in Silesia, now a part of Poland. The words were written by German Jesuits in the seventeenth century, who first published it in their *Münster Gesangbuch* in 1677, although the words have been found in a manuscript dating back to 1662.[7] Three verses in English by an anonymous translator appeared as *Fairest Lord Jesus* in Richard Sotorrs Willis's 1850 publication, *Church Chorals and Choir Studies*.

Four of its five verses were translated into English by Joseph A. Seiss in 1873. He called his translation *Beautiful Saviour*, and it is found under this title in many Lutheran hymnals. In most hymnals other than Lutheran ones, though, it is known as *Fairest Lord Jesus* with the words we all know. The UCC's hymnal, however, titles it *Beautiful Jesus*, in keeping with its "sensitivity to the use of the word 'Lord,'" thereby suggesting a picture of the "sweet Jesus" deplored by so much twentieth-century theology.

Yet just as the title captured their attention, so also editors did not allow the lyrics of this most popular of all hymns to escape unscathed, as issues of gender-inclusive language have been addressed. The gender-neutral rendition of *Fairest Lord Jesus* by the Presbyterians has an unexpectedly amusing aspect. The hymn begins:

> Fairest Lord Jesus, Ruler of all nature,
> O Thou of God and man the Son;
> Thee will I cherish, Thee will I honor,
> Thou, my soul's glory, joy and crown.

or in the Lutheran version:

> Beautiful Savior, King of Creation,
> Son of God and Son of Man!
> Truly I'd love Thee, truly I'd serve Thee,
> Light of my soul, my joy, my crown.

---

6. Julian, *A Dictionary of Hymnology*, 1016.
7. Bucke, *Companion to the Hymnal*, 170–71.

Both the Presbyterian and UCC hymnals felt obliged to change the last half of the opening couplet, although the latter rewrote it entirely:

> Beautiful Jesus, Head of all creation,
> God and blessed Mary's child.

On the other hand, the Presbyterians managed to create an almost heretically docetic statement with the words,

> Fairest Lord Jesus, Ruler of all nature
> O Thou of God to earth come down."

The amusing thing is that, had the Presbyterians translated the German original literally, as was done by the UCC, the gender specificity could have been avoided.

The opening couplet in the German is:

> Schönster Herr Jesu, Herrscher aller Herren,
> Gottes und Mariä Sohn;

the last half of which could have been translated, "O Thou of God and Mary the Son" or, as did the UCC, "God and the blessed Mary's child." In fact, "son" probably should have been used instead of "child" by the UCC, as no one has ever doubted that Mary's child, Jesus, was a boy.

The suspicion that this rendering might have been too "Romish" for these good Calvinistic editors is nullified by the almost parallel phraseology of the second verse of the Presbyterian version of *We All Believe in One True God* (Number 137 in *The Presbyterian Hymnal*), which begins, "We all believe in Jesus Christ, Son of God and Mary's son." As already noted, the latter half of this line would have fit the desired sense and meter in our hymn. Unfortunately, neither of these options was chosen for the Presbyterian version of *Fairest Lord Jesus*. Consequently, Presbyterians are now denied a marvelous statement in song of the Incarnation, being invited instead to entertain heresy, even if in today's climate churches seem reluctant to admit the existence of heretical ideas or statements. At the same time, the UCC is denied this favorite expression of the lordship of the Incarnated Christ.

Only the UCC has altered the remainder of this first verse. In accordance with its decision to avoid archaic language like "thee," "thine," "thou," "betide," and so on, these lines are rendered this way:

> I want to love you, praise and adore you,
> joy of my soul, so long desired.

With these words, all the "thou's" have certainly disappeared, but in its concern to change any possible hierarchical words it is questionable whether the last line sings the reign of Christ as clearly as does "Thou, my soul's glory, joy and crown."

The second and third verses as found in our hymnals have remained true to the original, for the most part. Certainly there are no differences caused by concerns about gender specific-language. It is curious, then, that the UCC has completely rewritten them. In what follows, Seiss' translation, that found in the Lutheran hymnal, is given, followed by that of the UCC's. Most readers will find Seiss' words quite like what they may have memorized as children. Verse two reads as follows:

> Fair are the meadows, Fair are the woodlands,
> Robed in the flowers of blooming spring;
> Jesus is fairer, Jesus is purer,
> He makes our sorrowing spirit sing.

In *The New Century Hymnal*, this verse is found as:

> Beautiful springtime, lovely, green and hopeful,
> all earth exhales its sweet perfume:
> Jesus is sweeter, Jesus is purer,
> sad hearts at this, rejoice and bloom.

It strikes me that no one would choose to sing this last in preference to Seiss' rendition.

The third verse is eerily similar. In Seiss' version:

> Fair is the sunshine, Fair is the moonlight,
> Bright the sparkling stars on high;
> Jesus shines brighter, Jesus shines purer
> Than all the angels in the sky.

In contrast to these popular words, the UCC hymnal reads:

> Beautiful sunshine, clear, so lovely, moonlight,
> stars shine like angels, ranked through space:
> Jesus shines brighter, Jesus shines clearer,
> in perfect beauty, love, and grace.

Only in the third line does one feel at home, and it strikes me as most unlikely that the UCC version of this extremely popular hymn will ever gain any traction.

Seiss had a fourth verse in his original, but it is almost never found in hymnals today. Following is Seiss' version of this verse:

> All fairest beauty, heavenly and earthly,
> Wondrously, Jesus, is found in Thee;
> None can be nearer, fairer or dearer,
> Than Thou, my Savior, art to me.

Failing to begin with either the word "fair" ("fairest") or "beautiful," it is perhaps easy to understand why this stanza has usually been omitted.

I think the UCC editors, consequently, deserve commendation for their inclusion of this verse, which they, like Seiss, place as their fourth with these words:

> All earthly beauty, all celestial radiance fade
> when compared to Jesus' face.
> Let me not cherish beauties that perish;
> let me this lovely good embrace.

Even these UCC editors, however, were unable to find a way to begin this verse with "Beautiful," as they did the other three. Nor does this latest attempt seem any more singable than was the earlier one. Furthermore, whether this retains the "nuance and intent" of the original adoration for the all-inclusive nature of Jesus in whom all other beauty finds fulfillment strikes me as highly questionable. Although it does bear a faint resemblance to the German, very little of the original English translation as proposed by Seiss is evident.

Seiss created a final verse, his fifth, out of phraseology from the first four. It is the fourth in many hymnals, as follows:

> Beautiful Savior, Lord of the nations,
> Son of God and Son of Man!
> Glory and honor, Praise, adoration
> Now and forevermore be Thine!

This glorious doxology in praise of the Incarnation is a fitting conclusion to the hymn, even if lacking in the original German. What is remarkable is that only the Baptists, Lutherans, and Methodists sing these words. One has the right to ask what is wrong with the others that they found it impossible to include this magnificent verse. It is the case, however, that by omitting it both Episcopalians and Presbyterians are able to avoid patriarchal language like the Son of God and Son of Man reference in this verse, although the Episcopalians retain this phrase in the first verse, an expression Presbyterians managed to avoid, as we have seen.

The final stanza in the German was omitted by Seiss from his first English version, and has generally been ignored ever since. In 2008, Christopher Dalitz prepared an arrangement of *Fairest Lord Jesus* set to its original baroque melody, and included his translation of the fifth verse.[8] Because of its different meter, his translation will not fit the melody usually associated with this hymn. Nevertheless, any treatment of this hymn should attempt to include the whole, so following is Dalitz's translation of verse 5:

> Beautiful Savior, thou art ever with us in the holy sacrament.
> Show us thy mercy, now and at our final end.
> Jesus we beg thee, now and at our final end.

This verse is a clear reference to I Corinthians 11:23–25, thereby introducing a new Scriptural idea, namely Paul's words of institution of the Lord's Supper:

> For I received from the Lord what I also handed on to you, that the Lord Jesus on the night when he was betrayed took a loaf of bread, and when he had given thanks, he broke it and said, "This is my body that is for you. Do this in remembrance of me." In the same way he took the cup also, after supper, saying, "This cup is the new covenant in my blood. Do this, as often as you drink it, in remembrance of me." (NRSV)

Seiss may simply have thought that the introduction of such a new concept destroyed the integrity of his Gospel-oriented rendition of the Incarnation as found in the other verses.

We see, then, that *Fairest Lord Jesus* has been the object of revision and change almost from its origin. As with any music, people have sung what appealed to them and changed or omitted what didn't. Thus one of the German verses only recently has been translated into English, and another was originally rendered into English but disappeared from the hymnals at an early date. Contemporary hymnals are making their changes based on the desire to eliminate gender specific-vocabulary,

---

8. Dalitz, http://music.dalitio.de/.

with unfortunate results for the Presbyterians and even more so for the members of the United Church of Christ. One can but hope that future publications of this hymn will be made with appropriate corrections.

Perhaps the popularity of this hymn has rested upon believers who appreciated the four seasons of the year, understanding and appreciating the end of winter and looking forward to the "blooming garb of Spring." Even those of us who are city dwellers can revel in the sights, sounds, and smells of "the meadows" and "the woodlands," although the light pollution all around us often precludes our enjoyment of "the twinkling starry host." Whatever the reason, however, *Fairest Lord Jesus* or *Beautiful Savior*, whichever you prefer, sung to the tune of CRUSADER HYMN, remains one of the most popular hymns in the repertoire of the Church. I suspect most in the UCC will simply ignore the changes in *The New Century Hymnal*.

Addendum

Schönster Herr Jesu[9]

1. Schönster Herr Jesu, Herrscher aller Herren,
    Gottes und Mariä Sohn!
    Dich will ich lieben, Dich will ich ehren,
    Meiner Seelen Freud' und Kron'!

2. Schön sind die Wälder, noch schöner sind die Felder
    In der schönen Frülingszeit!
    Jesus ist schöner, Jesus ist reiner,
    Der unser trauriges Herz erfreut!

3. Schön leucht der Monden, noch schöner leucht die Sonne
    Als die Sternlein allzumai!
    Jesus leucht schöner, Jesus ist reiner,
    Als die Engel im Himmelssaal.

4. All' die Schönheit Himmels und der Erden
    Ist nur gegen ihn als ein Schein!
    Keiner auf Erden uns lieber kann werden,
    Als der schönste Jesus mein!

5. Jesus ist wahrhaftig hoch von uns geliebet,
    Jesus ist wahrhaftig hoch gebenedeit!
    Jesus, wir bitten dich, sei uns gnädig
    Bis an unser letzte Zeit!

---

9. JCRH, *The Hymnal 1940 Companion*, 224: "... August Heinrich Hoffmann von Fallersleben recorded it in 1839, in the district of Glaz in Silesia, ... We quote from his *Schlesische Volkslieder*, 1842."

8

Hymn of Joy

THE *HYMN TO JOY* was an ode written in 1785 by the German poet and historian Friedrich Schiller with the title *An die Freude*. Schiller revised the ode in 1803, in the process creating the text used by Beethoven in 1805 for his Ninth Symphony. The *Ode to Joy* was adopted as Europe's anthem by the Council of Europe in 1972. In 2003, the European Union chose Beethoven's music for the poem as the EU anthem, but without its German lyrics because of the many different languages used within the European union. In 1908, Henry van Dyke (1852–1933) wrote the poem *Hymn of Joy* to the tune of Beethoven's music, which hymn we now know as *Joyful, Joyful, We Adore Thee*. Although there have also been changes to the rhythm of the music, that is not my concern in this work, so in what follows, I shall note only variations from the poem as van Dyke wrote it.[1]

Now to the language differences in the hymn itself. Some variations have no gender implications, so I will not spend much time on them. For instance, van Dyke began his poem for Beethoven's music this way:

> Joyful, joyful, we adore Thee,
> God of glory, Lord of love;
> Hearts unfold like flowers before Thee,
> Praising Thee their sun above.

The final phrase, "Praising Thee their sun above," has seen some changes. Whereas both the Episcopalian and Lutheran hymnals retain these words as written by van Dyke, Presbyterians sing, "Opening to the sun above," although by 1927 the Southern Presbyterians (PCUS) were singing, "Hail Thee as the sun above."[2] As can be seen in the addenda to this

---

1. See later, Addendum A at end of this chapter, for van Dyke's handwritten work.
2. Lingle, *The Presbyterian Hymnal*, 25.

chapter, all three originated with van Dyke at one time or another. By 1940, all Presbyterians were singing what is now found in their hymnal as well as in the Methodist, Baptist, and UCC hymnals: "Opening to the sun above" instead of "Praising Thee their sun above."[3] This change, however, has minimal theological implications and no gender significance.

For the third line of this first stanza, van Dyke wrote:

> Melt the clouds of sin and sadness;
> Drive the dark of doubt away.

The most recent Lutheran and Presbyterian hymnals have changed this last clause to: "Drive the gloom of doubt away," while the UCC hymnal has "Drive the storms of doubt away," readings which retain the theme but lose the alliteration of the original. Likewise, this also does not reflect a concern for gender neutrality, but probably results from racial interests to avoid any equation of evil with dark color. Presbyterian consistency in this racial arena is not maintained throughout the hymnal, however. For instance, the third line of the third verse of Martin Luther's *A Mighty Fortress* begins: "The Prince of darkness grim," with which all others but Lutherans and UCC agree. These last reflect a consistent concern for racial implications by changing the phrase to, "This world's prince may rage," in one version of the Lutheran hymnal and "Let this world's tyrant rage" in another, while the UCC changes it to, "The powers of evil grim."

But as racial language is not my concern either herein, let us return now to *Joyful, Joyful*, the very title of which has seen a change in *The New Century Hymnal*, where "*Thee*" is changed to "*You*," in deference to its commitment to the elimination of archaic language. That the stateliness of Beethoven's music might better suit the formal, dare we say archaic, language everyone else uses is a thought that apparently escaped the UCC editors! And every appearance of the "archaic" second person singular pronoun in the text of the hymn is similarly changed. In addition, their identification of the word "Lord" with patriarchal language that must be eliminated wherever possible causes them to change the second line to, "God of glory, God of love," thereby destroying van Dyke's alliteration, "Lord of love," and introducing a repetitive "God . . . God," which is hard to imagine as anyone's preference.

---

3. Sydnor, *Hymnal for Christian Worship*, 5.

We have discussed in earlier chapters how the omission of material is one effective way to neutralize offensive material, and this hymn has not escaped such a razor. The fourth verse, omitted by Episcopalians, Lutherans, and Baptists, but retained by Methodists, Presbyterians, and the UCC, was begun by van Dyke this way:

> Mortals join the mighty chorus
> Which the morning stars began;

words still employed by the UCC and Methodists. Presbyterians, however, by 1940, and still today, began singing "Mortals, join the happy chorus, etc."[4] One might enjoy speculating why Presbyterians, descended as they are from dour Scots Calvinists, would substitute "happy" for "mighty," especially since the latter would seem to fit their Sovereignty of God theology so much better, but again, such speculation has nothing to do with gender. Might it be part of the thinking of those moving to change the Eucharist invitation to invite communicants to "the joyful table" rather than to "the holy table?" It is as if Rudolph Otto's *The Idea of the Holy* has become irrelevant in today's world. But this is fodder for a different argument, so back to issues of gender.

As far as omissions are concerned, van Dyke's poem has been altered by almost everyone, with only the Methodists and UCC still singing all four stanzas. Presbyterians alone omit verse three, the last lines of which say:

> Thou our Father, Christ our Brother,
> All who live in love are Thine;
> Teach us how to love each other,
> Lift us to the joy divine.

By omitting this verse, Presbyterians dispense with these patriarchal references about the Fatherhood of God and brotherhood of man, and since Presbyterians alone in the next verse will join the "happy" chorus, they evidently felt no compunction to include the phrase "joy divine."

One wonders what van Dyke, staunch Presbyterian that he was, would have thought of this. When this hymn was first published as Number 115 in the Presbyterian *The Hymnal* of 1911, its title was *His Fatherhood and Love*.[5] Van Dyke himself was a clergyman who served

---

4. ibid.
5. Benson, *The Hymnal*, 115.

as pastor of New York City's Brick Presbyterian Church, a professor of English at Princeton University, and, by appointment of President Woodrow Wilson, U. S. Minister to the Netherlands and Luxembourg (1913–1916). He chaired the committee that wrote the first Presbyterian printed liturgy in 1906, *The Book of Common Worship*. Of the hymn *Joyful, Joyful, We Adore Thee*, he wrote:

> These verses are simple expressions of common Christian feelings and desires in the present time, hymns of today that may be sung together by people who know the thought of the age, and are not afraid that any truth of Science will destroy Religion, or any revolution on Earth overthrow the Kingdom of Heaven. Therefore, this is a Hymn of Trust, Joy and Hope.[6]

As we shall see in our examination of the next verse, that Presbyterians succeed in eliminating from his hymn the ancient Christian concept of the eternal Fatherhood of God is irony to the extreme.

In the same vein of thought, however, most will probably prefer the Presbyterian omission to what the UCC does to the last half of verse three:

> Loving Spirit, Father, Mother,
> all who love belong to you;
> Teach us how to love each other,
> by that love our joy renew.

That the English term "father" may be either gender specific or of a genderless, broader reference is generally understood, but no one doubts the gender-specific nature of the word "mother." Furthermore, that the simile "like a mother" to describe some actions of God may be found in the Bible is also the case. To make it a metaphor, however, is to introduce gender into one's understanding of the Godhead, a simply unacceptable act. To compound the enormity of the change made, "Mother" is substituted for "Christ our brother," thereby eliminating the crucial concept of the adoption of the believer in the risen Christ. The UCC would have done better to have followed the Presbyterian example and omitted this verse rather than perpetrate these changes.

Meanwhile, as already noted, Episcopalians, Lutherans, and Baptists omit verse four:

---

6. Van Dyke, *Thy Sea*, iii.

> Mortals, join the mighty chorus
> Which the morning star began;
> Father love is reigning o'er us,
> Brother love binds man to man.
> Ever singing, march we onward,
> Victors in the midst of strife,
> Joyful music leads us sunward
> In the triumph song of life.

These three denominations, having retained the language about Father love and the brotherhood of man in verse three, avoid any repetition of such patriarchal references by omitting the verse. But Presbyterians, for whom this is the third stanza, as well as Methodists and the UCC, who retain all four stanzas, avoid the gender references by substituting different words for the offensive material.

We have already discussed how Presbyterians became part of a "happy chorus" rather than a "mighty chorus" in the beginning of this final verse, the one omitted by Episcopalians, Lutherans, and Baptists. A possible reason for the decision to omit this stanza may be reflected in what Presbyterians, Methodists, and the UCC do to van Dyke's second line of the verse:

> Father love is reigning o'er us,
> Brother love binds man to man.

The former two change the first half of the line to the words,

> Love divine is reigning o'er us,

while the UCC has,

> Boundless love is reigning o'er us,

changes which by themselves are not too unfortunate. Both of these renditions, however, do eliminate the concept of the Fatherhood of God, which is such a part of Trinitarian theology. But as we continue our study of the hymns, we shall see constant changes of terms generic to the doctrine of the Trinity.

What happens in the second half of the line, however, can give one pause. Both Methodists and Presbyterians avoid any conception of the brotherhood of man, although at least the Methodists, as we have seen, have retained verse three with its third line:

> Thou our Father, Christ our Brother,
> all who live in love are thine.

Instead of any suggestion of the brotherhood of man, the Presbyterians reflect their predestinarianism with the words,

> Joining all in heaven's plan,

while Methodists remain quite Wesleyan with the words,

> binding all within its span,

where the "its" must refer to the earlier "Love divine." At least the UCC seems to capture something of the meaning of the original with its,

> reconciling race and clan.

It seems to me that these attempts at gender-neutral language illustrate the problem of the effort, as none have nearly the cachet of van Dyke's original,

> Brother love binds man to man.

Nor does "Love divine" or "Boundless love" have the same semantic field as "Father love."

Van Dyke avoided the use of the phrase "love divine" in this work, although it can be shown that he was familiar with it as useful for a hymn. For instance, in his letter of December 4, 1907, to Dr. Louis F. Benson about the publication of *Hymn of Joy* in the forthcoming hymnal of which the latter was editor, van Dyke wrote, "Thank you for setting 'O Love Divine' to 'Quebec.' I believe that hymn will make this tune its own."[7] This fine hymn, *O Love Divine, That Stooped to Share*, emphasizes the role of Jesus as pure expression of love and sharer of every human grief, as the source of courage to believers overwhelmed by life's sorrows and threats, and as the one whose constant nearness provides sustaining support every day. "Father love," on the other hand, suggests that the One whose mighty hand leads us and guards us and whose word is our law, is at the same time the One who saves us and refreshes us and fills our lives with love and grace. The connotations of the two phrases differ, in other words. I should think that one has the right to expect that those responsible for eliminating gender-specific language would attempt

---

7. Located by Deborah Cordonnier in a folder of letters between van Dyke and Benson in the Rare Books Room of the Library of Princeton Theological Seminary.

to retain the connotation of the expression considered problematical. Unfortunately, that does not seem to be a shared concern.

This examination of the contemporary publications of the hymn *Joyful, Joyful, We Adore Thee [You]* reveals that it is impossible to reconstruct what its recognized author, Henry van Dyke, actually wrote. One can but marvel at the willingness to change lyrics without even an acknowledgment to that effect. And some of these changes alter the theology of the author, what I would call a dastardly affront to the faith of believers dependent as they are upon the words in the hymnal for their singing.

For instance, Henry van Dyke, confirmed Calvinist and Presbyterian leader, raised Jack London's ire by writing,

> The Bible teaches that God owns the world. He distributes to every man according to his own good pleasure, conformably to general laws.[8]

To eliminate all of van Dyke's references to the Fatherhood of God, even to the extent of removing the theme itself from the hymn, is to rewrite his theology in an unacceptable manner. The same can be said about the removal of his strong affirmations of the believer's adoption into the risen Christ. Yet the elimination of these concepts is exactly what has been done, not only by his fellow Presbyterians, but by others as well.

This great hymn deserves better at the hand of today's editors.

---

8. Http://en.wikipedie.org/wiki/Henry_van_Dyke: "Van Dyke's 'Essays in Application' (1905) was quoted by Jack London in the dystopian novel 'The Iron Heel.' London disliked van Dyke's ideas, . . . Specifically, London took issue with van Dyke's statement, 'The Bible teaches etc. . . .'"

Addendum A

Handwritten Copy by Henry van Dyke

A Hymn of Joy
(Beethoven's Ninth Symphony)

Joyful, joyful, we adore Thee,
  God of glory, Lord of love;
Hearts unfold like flowers before Thee,
  Opening to the sun above.
Melt the clouds of sin and sadness;
  Drive the dark of doubt away;
Giver of immortal gladness,
  Fill us with the light of day.

All Thy works with joy surround Thee,
  Earth and heaven reflect Thy rays,
Stars and angels sing around Thee,
  Centre of unbroken praise.
Field and forest, vale and mountain,
  Flowery meadow, flashing sea,
Chanting bird and flowing fountain,
  Call us to rejoice in Thee.

Handwritten Copy by Henry van Dyke

page 2

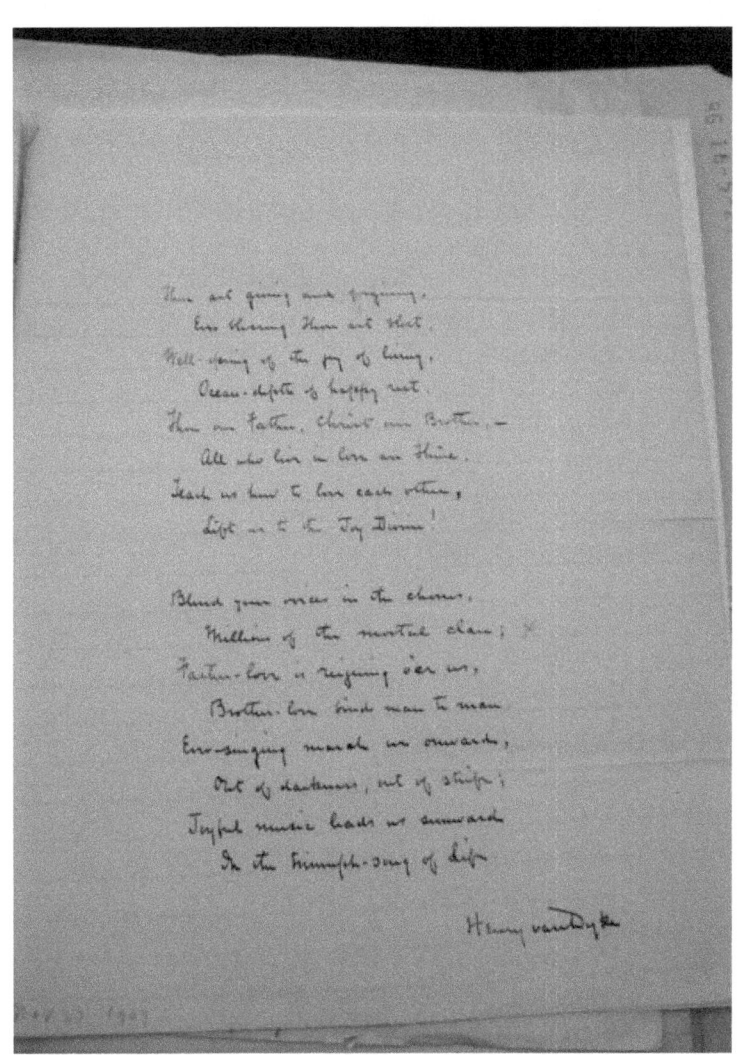

Addendum B

Proof Copy with van Dyke's Corrections

<u>Hymn of Joy</u>
with music of Beethoven's Ninth Symphony

Joyful, joyful, we adore Thee,
   God of glory, Lord of love;
Hearts unfold like flowers before Thee,
   ~~Hail Thee as the~~ sun above.
Melt the clouds of sin and sadness;
   Drive the dark of doubt away;
Giver of immortal gladness,
   Fill us with the light of day!

All Thy works with joy surround Thee,
   Earth and heaven reflect Thy rays,
Stars and angels sing around Thee,
   Center of unbroken praise:
Field and forest, vale and mountain,
   Blossoming meadow, flashing sea,
Chanting bird and flowing fountain,
   Call us to rejoice in Thee.

Thou art giving and forgiving,
   Ever blessing, ever blest,
Well-spring of the joy of living,
   Ocean-depth of happy rest!
Thou our Father, Christ our Brother,—
   All who live in love are Thine:
Teach us how to love each other,
   Lift us to the Joy Divine.

Enlargement of Corrections

by Henry van Dyke to Verse One

Hymn of Joy

Joyful, joyful, we adore Thee,
God of glory, Lord of love;
Hearts unfold like flowers before Thee,
~~Hail Thee as the sun above.~~
Melt the clouds of sin and sadness;
Drive the dark of doubt away;
Giver of immortal gladness,
Fill us with the light of day!

All Thy works with joy surround The[e]
Earth and heaven reflect Thy rays,
Stars and angels sing around Thee,
Center of unbroken praise;

9

The God of Abraham Praise

Few hymns create greater consternation within a congregation than *The God of Abraham Praise*, and this more for historical reasons than for those of inclusive language, although the latter concern has taken its toll. From its unusual origin to its variegated transmission, this hymn has been the source of confusion at almost every turn.

One of our hymnals, *The New Century Hymnal*, has even added verses in the interests both of the hymn's Hebrew origin and of gender neutrality. In deference to the former, the title is changed to *Yigdal Elohim Chai*, the first words of the Hebrew verse, with the usual title and initial words of the first line, "The God of Abraham Praise," in parentheses beneath. Then, to balance the first verse in English, a final verse is added that repeats the first exactly except for its beginning words, which are:

> The God of Sarah praise, etc.

In this case, we see gender balancing by the UCC rather than the removal of gender specificity. This tactic is seldom encountered elsewhere, however, as it tends to magnify differences of gender rather than eliminate them.

There are other interesting things about this hymn, however. Its first version was by Thomas Olivers, who wrote it after hearing Meyer Lyon, Cantor in the Great Synagogue, Duke's Place, London, sing the *Yigdal*, or Hebrew confession of faith. The *Yigdal* is believed to have been written in 1404 by Daniel ben Judah, a Jewish judge in Rome, and is based on the thirteen creeds of Moses Maimonides (*c*.1130–*c*.1204).[1] These can be summarized as follows:

> 1. The *Yigdal* (יגדל) in English: (1) Exalted be the Living God and praised, He exists - unbounded by time is His existence; (2) He is One - and there is no unity like

1. Belief in the existence of a Creator and Providence;

2. Belief in His unity;

3. Belief in His incorporeality;

4. Belief in His eternity;

5. Belief that to Him alone is worship due;

6. Belief in the words of the prophets;

7. Belief that Moses was the greatest of all prophets;

8. Belief in the revelation of the Law to Moses at Sinai;

9. Belief in the immutability of the Revealed Law;

10. Belief that God is omniscient; and

11. Belief in the resurrection of the dead.

Olivers was so impressed by the solemn, plaintive Hebrew melody that he determined to write a hymn to Lyon's tune. Sometime between 1763 and 1770, he took the words of the *Yigdal*, gave them a Christian setting as far as possible, and set them to the tune which he called LEONI, after Meyer Lyon. It first appeared as a tract, the fourth edition in 1772 being the first to be dated, and after eight editions it passed into John Wesley's *Pocket Hymnbook for the Use of Christians of All Denominations* (1785), whereupon it became extremely popular in Methodist circles.[2]

Olivers wrote the hymn with twelve verses, but, not unexpectedly, few contemporary hymnals preserve the entire work.[3] Although the

---

His Oneness - Inscrutable and infinite is His Oneness; (3) He has no semblance of a body nor is He corporeal - nor has His holiness any comparison; (4) He preceded every being that was created - the First, and nothing precedes His precedence; (5) Behold! He is Master of the universe to every creature - He demonstrates His greatness and His sovereignty; (6) He granted His flow of prophecy - to His treasured, splendid people; (7) In Israel, none like Moses arose again - a prophet who perceived His vision clearly; (8) God gave His people a Torah of truth - by means of His prophet, the most trusted of His household; (9) God will never amend nor exchange His law - for any other one, for all eternity; (10) He scrutinizes and knows our hiddenmost secrets - He perceives a matter's outcome at its inception; (11) He recompenses man with kindness according to his deed - He places evil on the wicked according to his wickedness; (12) By the End of Days He will send our Messiah - to redeem those longing for His final salvation; (13) God will revive the dead in His abundant kindness - Blessed is His praised Name.

2. Dearmer, *Songs*, 218.

3. See Appendix A at the end of this chapter for the twelve verses as written by Thomas Olivers.

Methodists were still printing all twelve verses in 1900, surprisingly, today only the Lutheran hymnal prints all twelve, with the first four verses within the music and the remainder as additional stanzas. The first three verses all begin with the words, "The God of Abraham praise," and of those hymnals that follow Olivers' words, again only the Lutherans sing these three verses, both Methodists and Episcopalians skipping from verse one to verse four. Having said this, however, what about other hymnals?

Upon addressing the Presbyterian, Baptist, and UCC presentations of the hymn, *The God of Abraham Praise*, the first notable difference is that the lyrics are not attributed to Thomas Olivers at all, but rather to Max Landsberg and Newton Mann! Both of these worthies worked in Rochester, New York, during the latter part of the nineteenth century, Mann as Pastor of the First Unitarian Church from 1870 to 1888 and Landsberg as Chief Rabbi of Temple Berith Kodesh from 1871 to 1911. The Temple and the Unitarian Church shared joint Thanksgiving services, and the two clergymen collaborated on a new translation and versification of the *Yigdal* into four verses that they called *Praise to the Living God*, with the following first verse:

> Praise to the living God! All praised be His Name,
> who was and is—and is to be, for aye the same!
> The One Eternal God ere aught that now appears:
> The First, the Last, beyond all thought His timeless years![4]

Dr. William C. Gannett, Newton Mann's successor as Pastor of the Unitarian Church, recast the work, omitted one verse, changed its title to *The God of Abraham Praise*, and the beginning lyrics from "Praise to the living God" to the same words as the title. By 1940, these, then, were the three verses identified by Presbyterians, Baptists, and UCC as this particular hymn.

Following is the first verse of the recast hymn:

> The God of Abraham praise, All praised be His Name,
> Who was, and is, and is to be, And still the same!
> The one eternal God, Ere aught that now appears;
> The First, the Last: Beyond all thought His timeless years!

---

4. See Appendix B at the end of this chapter for the four verses as created by Landsberg and Mann.

As members of the Calvinist churches sang these words by Landsberg and Mann, it is a simple matter to imagine the confusion caused as Episcopalians, Lutherans, and Methodists sang the same hymn with the following by Olivers as its first verse:

> The God of Abraham praise, who reigns enthroned above;
> Ancient of everlasting days, and God of Love;
> Jehovah, great I AM! By earth and Heav'n confessed;
> I bow and bless the sacred Name forever blessed.

Both groups, however, sang their respective words to the tune LEONI, so at least Meyer Lyon's work remained consistent. The exception to this situation may be found in the Methodist hymnals of 1935 and 1964, which deserted Olivers for the Landsberg/Mann version. *The United Methodist Hymnal* of 1989, however, returned to the Olivers version.[5]

For a number of decades in the twentieth century, the Christianized musical versions of the *Yigdal* were known as *The God of Abraham Praise* and were sung in these two different redactions, without any interaction between them save for the exception just noted. Baptists, Presbyterians, and those churches that now comprise the UCC sang the words of Landsberg and Mann, while Methodists, Lutherans, and Episcopalians sang those of Olivers. The only difference within this latter group in today's hymnals involves which of the twelve verses are to be included in the hymnal. While Lutherans manage to include all twelve verses, the Methodists, for whom the hymn was originally written, confine themselves to four verses now, namely the first, fourth, sixth, and tenth. The Episcopalians, on the other hand, manage to include five verses in their hymnal, again the first and the fourth, but in addition, the seventh and the twelfth along with the tenth.

Olivers' *The God Of Abraham Praise* by verses

Olivers	Methodist	Episcopalian	Lutheran
1	1	1	1
2			2
3			3
4	2	2	4
5			5

5. Bucke, *Companion to the Hymnal*, 356.

The God of Abraham Praise 91

Olivers	Methodist	Episcopalian	Lutheran
6	3		6
7		3	7
8			8
9			9
10	4	4	10
11			11
12		5	12

This happy distinction between the Olivers and the Landsberg/Mann versions continued until 1989 and the appearance of the "blue" Presbyterian Hymnal. For reasons unexplained, the editors of this most recent Presbyterian form of the hymn have chosen to replace the Landsberg/Mann first verse with that by Olivers, thereby confusing all those members who were accustomed to singing the former. Like previous Presbyterian hymnals, however, only two more verses were included for the hymn, and these were the last two of the Landsberg/Mann version, without any admixture from Olivers. Thus we find a griffin-like hymn, with the head from one version and the body from another! And this change precedes any attention from those concerned about inclusive language.

Yet even when inserting this first verse from Olivers' version, which has no problems associated with gender identification, one encounters a confusing alteration perpetrated by the Presbyterians. As noted earlier, Olivers wrote as the last line in this verse:

> I bow and bless the sacred Name forever blessed.

Both Episcopalians and Presbyterians change the "I" to "We," a laudable change to make the line more encompassing, but Presbyterians introduce a comma and substitute a pronoun for the definite article, reading the line as:

> We bow before Your holy name, Forever blesst.

While the gender-neutral second person pronoun does add a personal element to the relationship between believer and the Divine, it also invites a question as to the identity of the "Forever blesst." Is it God, as suggested by the "Your?" Is it the "sacred Name," as clearly meant in Olivers' original? Or is it an ungrammatical but poetically licensed reference to the "We" that begins the clause? What unnecessary confusion caused by the simple substitution of a pronoun for an article and the addition of a comma, a confusion that calls to mind the recent popular work by Lynn Truss, *Eats, Shoots & Leaves*, to which reference is made in the Introduction.

A change in these last two verses, however, is much less poetic. Landsberg/Mann repeats the line,

> Who was, and is, and is to be, for aye the same!

placing it both as the second line of the first verse and the concluding line of the hymn. For some reason, this line seems to have displeased the latest Presbyterian editors, who, having eliminated its first appearance by inserting Olivers' words for the first verse, change the last line of the third and final verse to the words that ended the original first verse,

> The first, the last, beyond all thought, And still the same!

To eliminate the closing phrase, "His timeless years," a comma has been inserted and the phrase is replaced by, "And still the same!" Thus, what had been a twice-repeated poetic statement of the eternal nature of God has disappeared, replaced by a more prosaic one that injects subjective and temporal elements into the idea.

The Hebrew transliteration of the first two lines of the *Yigdal* are used by the UCC as the first verse of their version, as follows:

> Yigdal Elohim chai v'yishtabach
> nimtza v'ein at el m'tziuto.
> Echad v'ein yachid k'yichudo
> n'elam v'gam ein sof l'achduto.

This is a nice touch to introduce the very Hebraic nature of both the words and the melody of this stately hymn.

In addition to these changes, the Presbyterians and the UCC have also made more problematical gender alterations involving language about God. Although the New Revised Standard Version (NRSV) is the text of Scripture on which both depend, neither is willing to follow its format when hymns talk about the Divine. Landsberg/Mann wrote both the second and the third verses in the third person, giving them a strong sense of majesty in their references to God. Thus,

> "His spirit floweth free . . . He speaketh still. . . . Established is His law . . . He hath eternal life . . . His love . . . All praised be His name."

In all of these places, the UCC retains the third person by using "God" or "God's," thereby becoming as repetitive as some contemporary liturgies. The Presbyterians, on the other hand, have changed the "He" and "His" to "You" and "Yours," to read,

> "Your spirit still flows free . . . You speak still . . . Established is Your law . . . You have eternal life . . . Your love . . . We praise your holy name."

By making these changes, both have rendered this hymn gender neutral, although a bit boringly by the UCC, while the Presbyterians have actually made it more personal, at the expense of its original grandeur. Only the Baptists continue to sing the Landsberg/Mann version as it was originally published in its Gannett revision.

As for what has been done to Olivers' work, both Episcopalians and Methodists have "sanitized" those verses they include, but in different ways. Both preserve Olivers' fourth verse,

> He by Himself has sworn; I on His oath depend,
> I shall, on eagle's wings upborne, to Heav'n ascend.
> I shall behold His face; I shall His power adore,
> And sing the wonders of His grace forevermore.

Where the Methodists address issues of gender in lines one and three, however, the Episcopalians address the issue of individualism versus the corporate body, as follows:

> Meth: The great I AM has sworn, I on this oath depend.
> Epis: He by himself hath sworn: we on his oath depend;

and for the third line,

> Meth: I shall behold God's face; I shall God's power adore,
> Epis: we shall behold his face, we shall his power adore.

Each version of these verses thereby is made less personal than Olivers' original, the Methodists doing so by removing the "I-his" relationship and the Episcopalians by subsuming the individual "I" within the corporate "we."

Throughout what they print of this hymn, both remain consistent to this principle, with the Methodists regularly removing the third person masculine singular pronoun when used to refer to the Divine and the Episcopalians retaining it but always substituting "we" for "I." The change in personal emphasis by the Episcopalians may be illustrated by the second line of this verse when Methodists sing,

> I shall on eagle wings upborne to heaven ascend,

where the former sing,

> We shall on eagles wings ascend.

The plural "we" diminishes the personal element somewhat, especially as this refers to rising to heaven and to seeing God, which is the subject of the next line. At the same time, by consistently changing the "His" to something else, the Methodists diminish the sense of a personal relationship between the singer and another, in this case God.

Another interesting change made by the Episcopalians involves the use of the word "Jehovah," the mistaken Hebrew form of God's name. This word for the name of God occurs in both the first and the tenth verses. Whereas in verse one Methodists sing,

> Jehovah, great I AM, By earth and heaven confessed,

Episcopalians sing,

> The Lord, the great I AM, by earth and heaven confessed,

a change that threatens to render meaningless the following line,

> We bow and bless the sacred Name forever blest.

Having eliminated the name of God, to what does the phrase "the sacred Name" refer?

The change in the tenth verse is less problematical, as "Jehovah, Father, great I AM" becomes for the Episcopalians "Eternal Father, great I AM." It is both interesting and commendatory to note the concern by these latter editors for removing this inaccurate form, Jehovah, for the Hebrew tetragrammaton YHWH (יהוה), the four-letter name of God.

At the same time, while Episcopalians and Methodists were expressing their concerns for gender, individualism, and Hebrew accuracy, the

Lutherans were printing all twelve verses of Oliver's version with very few changes, as seen in the following chart:

Olivers' Version	Lutheran Hymnal
3/2 happy days	3/2 pilgrim days
3/3 He calls a worm his friend	3/3 He deigns to call me friend
7/3 His kingdom still maintains	7/3 His kingdom He maintains
8/4 And sing, in song	8/4 And sing the songs
10/3 His prints of love	10/3 his wounds of love
10/4 the slaughtered Lamb	10/4 The Paschal Lamb

These six changes in the twelve verses of the hymn show wonderful restraint, especially since few of them are significant. By the way they eliminated the worm reference in verse three, the Lutherans personalized the theology of adoption while foregoing Olivers' dramatic expression of the depravity of human kind.[6] Such personalization is further emphasized in verse ten by changing "prints of love" to "wounds of love," thereby reminding the singer of the motivation underlying Christ's stigmata. The change of "slaughtered" to "Paschal" further stresses this emphasis upon the sacrifice of Christ.

The current confusion associated with this hymn, then, owes less to concerns about the language of gender inclusiveness than is often the case. Only the Methodists, Presbyterians, and UCC, in fact, have chosen to make their respective versions gender inclusive. The Lutheran and Episcopalian editors, instead, have addressed other issues, apparently having decided to honor the Jewish basis of the hymn by leaving its masculine pronouns to refer to the Divine antecedent. Furthermore, originally different hymns are in play, and only two of the hymnals remain relatively faithful to their origins, the Lutherans to the Olivers version and the Baptists to the Landsberg/Mann version. While the Episcopalians and Methodists pick and choose from the Olivers version

---

6. To some degree, this parallels the standard amendment of Isaac Watts' *Alas! And Did My Savior Bleed* where verse one is changed from "Would he devote that sacred head for such a worm as I" to " . . . for sinners such as I."

and the UCC makes its changes in the Landsberg/Mann original, the Presbyterians have gone their own way by creating a mixture of the two versions. One must hope that the editors of future versions of these and other hymnals will consult each other before attempting new editions of such an inspiring hymn.

Addendum A

Olivers' Twelve Verses[7]

1. The God of Abraham praise, who reigns enthroned above;
   Ancient of everlasting days, and God of love;
   Jehovah, great I AM! by earth and heav'n confessed;
   I bow and bless the sacred Name forever blessed.

2. The God of Abraham praise, at Whose supreme command
   From earth I rise—and seek the joys at His right hand.
   I all on earth forsake, Its wisdom, fame, and power;
   And Him my only Portion make, my Shield and Tower.

3. The God of Abraham praise, whose all sufficient grace
   Shall guide me all my happy days, in all my ways.
   He calls a worm His friend, He calls Himself my God!
   And He shall save me to the end, thro' Jesus' blood.

4. He by Himself has sworn; I on His oath depend,
   I shall, on eagle's wings upborne, to Heav'n ascend.
   I shall behold His face; I shall His power adore,
   And sing the wonders of His grace forevermore.

5. Tho' nature's strength decay, and earth and hell withstand,
   To Canaan's bounds I urge my way, at His command.
   The wat'ry deep I pass, with Jesus in my view;
   And thro' the howling wilderness my way pursue.

6. The goodly land I see, with peace and plenty bless'd;
   A land of sacred liberty, and endless rest.
   There milk and honey flow, and oil and wine abound,

---

7. Julian, *A Dictionary of Hymnology*, 1150.

      And trees of life forever grow with mercy crowned.

7. There dwells the Lord our King, the Lord our righteousness,
    Triumphant o'er the world and sin, the Prince of Peace;
    On Sion's sacred height His kingdom still maintains,
    And glorious with His saints in light forever reigns.

8. He keeps His own secure, He guards them by His side,
    Arrays in garments, white and pure, His spotless bride:
    With streams of sacred bliss, with groves of living joys —
    With all the fruits of Paradise, He still supplies.

9. Before the great Three-One they all exulting stand;
    And tell the wonders He hath done through all their land;
    The list'ning spheres attend, and swell the growing fame;
    And sing, in songs which never end, the wondrous Name.

10. The God Who reigns on high the great archangels sing,
    and "Holy, holy, holy!" cry, "Almighty King!
    Who was, and is, the same, and evermore shall be:
    Jehovah—Father—great I AM, we worship Thee!"

11. Before the Savior's face the ransomed nations bow;
    O'er whelmed at His almighty grace, forever new;
    He shows His prints of love—they kindle to a flame!
    And sound thro' all the worlds above the slaughtered Lamb.

12. The whole triumphant host give thanks to God on high;
    "Hail Father, Son, and Holy Ghost," they ever cry.
    Hail, Abraham's God, and mine! (I join the heav'nly lays,)
    All might and majesty are Thine, and endless praise.

Addendum B

Landsberg/Mann Version[8]

1. Praise to the living God! All praised be His Name,
    who was and is, and is to be, for aye the same!
    The One Eternal God ere aught that now appears:
    the First, the Last, beyond all thought His timeless years!

2. Formless, all lovely forms, declare His loveliness;
    holy, no holiness of earth can His express.
    Lo, He is Lord of all, Creation speaks His praise;
    And, everywhere, above, below, His will obeys.

3. His spirit floweth free, high surging where it will;
    in prophet's word He spake of old, and speaketh still.
    Established is His law, and peerless it shall stand,
    deep writ upon the human heart, on sea or land.

4. Eternal life hath He implanted in the soul;
    His love shall be our strength and stay while ages roll.
    Praise to the living God! All praised be His Name,
    who was, and is, and is to be, for aye the same.

---

8. http://www.oremus.org/hymnal/p/p102.html.

10

Make Love Not War

Words like "soldiers" and "war" conjure up images of troops in battle, armed with deadly weapons. Hymns with terms like these used to be a regular part of the American worship service. Such a vision of Christian faith, however, with its militaristic language, was seemingly unacceptable to many of those concerned about gender-specific language in the hymns of the church. Apparently, some of those so worried in the 1960s and 1970s associated war and the words of war with masculinity: in other words, a male enterprise, and this at the same time that opposition to the Vietnam War was becoming the opinion of the majority of folk in the U.S. This position seems to have become the dominant attitude for the remainder of the twentieth century.

As a result, some popular hymns that use the language of war to describe the Christian struggle against evil have been acceptable candidates for omission from the contemporary hymnals we are examining. Consequently, as we have moved into a time when women are found in combat, some even flying fighter planes into war zones, the hymnals of our mainline Protestant churches have been removing such images from the songs sung by believers. By doing so, questionable theological statements are also being made.

For instance, both Presbyterians and the UCC have quit singing *Onward, Christian Soldiers*, while only the outrage among church-goers at its proposed omission caused the committee overseeing the new Methodist hymnal to change its decision and include it.[1] It is as if the Presbyterians and the UCC were saying that, although dealing with sin may be a struggle, it is no war. Furthermore, since at that time in the nation's history women were not allowed in combat, to sing of war may

---

1. "New Methodist Hymnal Is Shorn of Stereotypes," *The New York Times*; June 20, 1989.

have seemed to smack of gender discrimination. Yet the popularity of this hymn remains unabated.

Written in 1865, its author, Sabine Baring-Gould, made the following comment about its composition:

> Whit-Monday [*the day after Pentecost*] is a great day for school festivals in Yorktown. One Whit-Monday, thirty years ago, it was arranged that our school should join forces with that of a neighboring village. I wanted the children to sing when marching from one village to another, but couldn't think of anything quite suitable; so I sat up at night, resolved that I would write something myself. *Onward, Christian Soldiers* was the result.[2]

Several years after its composition, Sir Arthur S. Sullivan, of Gilbert and Sullivan fame, wrote a new tune for it that he called ST. GERTRUDE. With this new tune, *Onward, Christian Soldiers* rapidly became one of the most popular of hymns sung worldwide.

It was one of the hymns chosen by Winston Churchill to be sung at the worship service on the battleship HMS Prince of Wales when he and President Franklin Roosevelt met in 1941 to agree on the Atlantic Charter. In the words of Prime Minister Churchill:

> We sang *Onward, Christian Soldiers* indeed, and I felt that this was no vain presumption, but that we had the right to feel that we were serving a cause for the sake of which a trumpet has sounded from on high. When I looked upon that densely packed congregation of fighting men of the same language, of the same faith, of the same fundamental laws, of the same ideals . . . it swept across me that here was the only hope, but also the sure hope, of saving the world from measureless degradation.[3]

The song has been sung at a host of funerals as well, including that of President Dwight D. Eisenhower at the National Cathedral, Washington, DC, on March 31, 1969.

Even when the Presbyterians and UCC did sing this hymn, however, they sang the four-verse version still enjoyed by Lutherans that omits the second of the five-verse version sung by both Methodists and Episcopalians. This second verse affirms the church in the following powerful words:

2. Online: http://songsandhymns.org/hymns/detail/onward-christian-soldiers, 2.

3. Collins, *Stories Behind the Hymns That Inspire America*, 153–154; Online: cited in Wikipedia article, "Onward, Christian Soldiers."

> At the sign of triumph, Satan's host doth flee;
> on then, Christian soldiers, on to victory!
> Hell's foundations quiver at the shout of praise;
> brothers, lift your voices, loud your anthems raise.

Although Episcopalians change the last line to "Christians, lift your voices, etc.," the Methodist committee must have still been shell-shocked by its member outrage, as a consequence failing to make the usual gender-neutral change. Why Presbyterians, Lutherans, and the UCC have resisted the singing of the church's attack on Hell itself must remain a mystery, unless the reference to the Matthean version of Peter's Confession (Matthew 16:13–20), with its promise to Peter and gift of the keys of heaven to the church, was considered to be just too papish.

Interestingly, Baptists sing this second verse in their four-verse version of the hymn, but omit the fourth verse:

> Crowns and thrones may perish, Kingdoms rise and wane,
> But the Church of Jesus Constant will remain;
> Gates of hell can never 'Gainst that Church prevail.
> We have Christ's own promise, And that cannot fail.

Thus the second of the unambiguous references to the account of Peter's Confession in the Gospel of Matthew is omitted by the Baptist editors. At least, however, the hymn is sung, something members of the Presbyterian and UCC churches can no longer do.

Stand Up, Stand Up for Jesus, a hymn with an admittedly weak tune, has suffered the same fate as *Onward, Christian Soldiers*, nor has anyone tried to write a new tune for it. Recalling the argument of Ephesians 6:10–17 about "putting on the whole armor of God," it continues to be sung by all save the Presbyterians and UCC, both having omitted it from their latest hymnals. Ironically, the author, George Duffield, Jr., was the son and grandson of Presbyterian ministers, and himself graduated from Union Theological Seminary. He wrote the hymn with six stanzas, but only four continue to be sung, the second and the fifth generally being omitted. And in none of those who continue to sing it is Duffield's fifth stanza found:

> Stand up, stand up for Jesus, each soldier to his post!
> Close up the broken column, and shout through all the host:
> Make good the loss so heavy, in those that still remain,
> And prove to all around you that death itself is gain.

A moving and thrilling stanza indeed!

In addition to the questions surrounding warlike imagery among contemporary editors, this verse adds the idea that the struggle against evil also involves casualties. That the line may be broken and need to be "closed up" introduces the dangerous idea that to oppose evil may lead to death, while the verse ends with the clause "that death itself is gain," distinctly unpopular concepts today. In our current culture, dedicated as it is to everlasting youth, physical vitality, and immediate gratification, death whether by natural causes or otherwise would seem to be a forbidden subject and certainly no gain. Who, then, needs a hymn that includes a stanza like this? Certainly not Presbyterians and the UCC, while all others when singing the hymn happily omit the verse.

Thus an additional hymn proclaiming the victorious march of the army of God has begun to disappear, as two of our churches no longer sing these words:

> Stand up, stand up for Jesus, Ye soldiers of the cross;
> Lift high His royal banner, It must not suffer loss:
> From vict'ry unto vict'ry His army shall He lead,
> Till every foe is vanquished, and Christ is Lord indeed.

This is a hymn that urges the believer to welcome the opportunity to attack whenever evil is perceived. It reminds one of the words of French revolutionary Georges Jacques Danton in a 1792 speech, often quoted by World War II American General George Patton, "De l'audace, encore de l'audace, toujours de l'audace" ("Audacity, more audacity, always audacity"). But I think it safe to say that any reminder of General Patton becomes a candidate for elimination from a hymnal in today's world. Certainly the Presbyterians and the UCC have opted to eliminate it.

Another hymn based on Ephesians 6:10–17, and with the word "soldiers" in the title, *Soldiers of Christ, Arise*, has not faired as well as the two we have discussed so far. It has been retained by Methodists and Episcopalians alone. Written by Charles Wesley in 1747 and originally entitled *The Whole Armor of God*, it initially appeared as a sixteen-stanza hymn in the 1749 publication *Hymns and Sacred Poems*. When it appeared in John Wesley's *Collection of Hymns for the People Called Methodists*, published in 1780, it had been reduced to twelve verses.[4] The three-stanza version that was most commonly sung dates from 1847, and consists of Wesley's first two verses plus a third verse made up of the first two lines from Wesley's fourth and twelfth stanzas.

---

4. Bucke, *Companion to the Hymnal*, 376.

The Episcopalians in their latest hymnal have moved in their own way to combine verses for this hymn. Fitting the hymn to a different tune, SILVER STREET rather than the more generally used DIADEMATA, they have created a five-stanza hymn. The first two stanzas are made by dividing Wesley's first stanza in half, while the third stanza consists of the first two lines from Wesley's second stanza. The fourth stanza is made up of the first two lines from the twelfth stanza, and the Episcopalians' last verse is made up of the final two lines from Wesley's second stanza. Thus have the Episcopalians created their own version of *Soldiers of Christ, Arise*.

The Methodists, the other church still singing this hymn, have been more straightforward in their contemporary treatment of Wesley's original. They sing a four-stanza version consisting of Wesley's first two verses, followed by his eighth verse, and ending with the twelfth verse. In this way, the Methodists have both corrected previous line-splitting and avoided the creation of verses by the combination of lines from several of Wesley's original stanzas.

Nor has such treatment by omission been restricted to Wesley's work, for even Isaac Watts, the father of hymn-writing in the English language, has had some of his popular hymns eliminated. In 1709, he penned his hymn, *Am I a Soldier of the Cross?* to follow a sermon on I Corinthians 16:13:

> Watch ye, stand fast in the faith, quit you like men, be strong (KJV),

rendered in the NRSV as

> Keep alert, stand firm in your faith, be courageous, be strong.

In this case, only the Baptists and Methodists have retained the hymn, and only the latter print all six verses. Thus the Baptists raise the question, "Am I a soldier of the Cross?" but miss the glorious conclusion of the final two verses still sung by the Methodists:

> Thy saints in all this glorious war shall conquer, though they die;
> they see the triumph from afar, by faith they bring it nigh.

> When that illustrious day shall rise, and all thy armies shine
> in robes of victory through the skies, the glory shall be thine.

Once again we see the omission of a hymn detailing the serious nature of the conflict between the people of Christ and the forces of evil, where the fact of death in the struggle is admitted and the victory anticipated in the future. In a culture like ours, committed as it is to rampant consumerism, the acknowledgment of death and future satisfaction would seem to be unacceptable and certainly not a matter for inclusion in our hymnals.

An omitted hymn I really miss, but one still sung by the Lutherans, and only them, is another militaristic song, *The Son of God Goes Forth to War*, with its marvelous refrain, "Who follows in His train?" When this question is first asked, the hymn continues:

> Who best can drink his cup of woe, Triumphant over pain,
> Who patient bears his cross below, He follows in His train.

Had this hymn been retained, gender neutrality would have required a change of the masculine singular personal pronoun in the final clause. But in any event, this might be too much pain for contemporary members of mainline churches, who often do not seem to be all that much into cross-bearing.

At the same time, it is noteworthy that, when they did sing this hymn, Presbyterians omitted the third verse, leaving its doctrine of election completely to the Lutherans:

> A glorious band, the chosen few On whom the Spirit came,
> Twelve valiant saints, their hope they knew, And mocked
>   the cross and flame:
> They met the tyrant's brandished steel, the lion's gory mane;
> They bowed their necks the death to feel: Who follows
>   in their train?

This is certainly election, and in words that are stark indeed!

By omitting this hymn, the other churches leave to the Lutherans the final magnificent and historically gender-inclusive verse:

> A noble army, men and boys, The matron and the maid,
> Around the Savior's throne rejoice, in robes of light arrayed;
> They climbed the steep ascent of heaven Through peril, toil,
>   and pain;
> O God, to us may grace be given To follow in their train!

One cannot sing such words and be comfortable in the face of the many expressions heard today which reflect a shallow understanding of the paralyzing power of sin, accompanied as they often are by equally shallow descriptions of grace, what Dietrich Bonhöffer called "cheap grace."

As an aside, I wonder whether these hymn editors were gripped by the same fever that laid hold of U.S. Representative Andy Jacobs of Indiana a few years ago when he briefly sponsored a bill to scrap *The Star-Spangled Banner* with its blood-thirsty third verse, which is proud to report, "their blood has washed out their foul footsteps' pollution." Nor could any refuge save "the hireling and slave from the terror of flight or the gloom of the grave." The French also recently considered rewriting *La Marseillaise* with its stirring chorus call to arms, "to drench our fields with the foe's tainted blood."[5] Apparently the leaders of our mainline churches were caught up in the same sentiment about militaristic language, leading them to omit those hymns that use graphically war-like language.

Whatever may have been the reasons, and there probably were more than one, the result has been that many of those hymns that most vividly describe war with the forces of evil are no longer part of mainline church hymnody. That the church has a centuries-old vocabulary that is being forgotten may help explain the confusion many believers feel upon being confronted with the Islamic concept of *jihad*, or war against evil. In many ways, this concept is nothing but the Muslim adaptation of an even more ancient Christian concept. For Christians to think the word can only apply to acts of terrorism is to reveal a woeful lack of theological understanding. At the same time, such a lack of understanding may simply reflect a diminishing sense of the seriousness of the struggle against evil, especially when one considers how, since 9/11, such language has often been equated with nothing more than opposition to *al-Qaida* and Taliban terrorism.

Does this lack of understanding explain the disappearance of hymns that contain terms like "soldiers" or "war," or does the disappearance of these hymns help explain, among many Christians today, the apparently diminished understanding of the intensity of the conflict with evil? Or is this a chicken-and-egg question? In any event, it is enough to note that the desire to eliminate militaristic language from our hymns has accompanied the concern to eliminate gender-specific language. Some great hymns are consequently disappearing from the repertoire.

---

5. Kilpatrick, "Save the Marseillaise and The Star-Spangled Banner!" *The State*; unknown issue. "To drench etc." = "Marchons, marchons! Qu'un sang impur abreuve nos sillons!"

Addendum A

Soldiers of Christ, Arise

Charles Wesley's Twelve Verse Version[6]

1. Soldiers of Christ, arise, and put your armor on,
    strong in the strength which God supplies through His eternal Son.
    Strong in the Lord of hosts, and in His mighty power,
    Who in the strength of Jesus trusts is more than conqueror.

2. Stand then in His great might, with all His strength endued,
    But take, to arm you for the fight, the panoply of God;
    That, having all things done, and all your conflicts passed,
    Ye may o'ercome through Christ alone and stand entire at last.

3. Stand then against your foes, in close and firm array;
    Legions of wily fiends oppose throughout the evil day.
    But meet the sons of night, and mock their vain design,
    Armed in the arms of heavenly light, of righteousness divine.

4. Leave no unguarded place, no weakness of the soul,
    Take every virtue, every grace, and fortify the whole;
    Indissolubly joined, to battle all proceed;
    But arm yourselves with all the mind that was in Christ, your Head.

5. But, above all, lay hold on faith's victorious shield;
    Armed with that adamant and gold, be sure to win the field:
    If faith surround your heart, Satan shall be subdued,
    Repelled his every fiery dart, and quenched with Jesus' blood.

6. Jesus hath died for you! What can His love withstand?
    Believe, hold fast your shield, and who shall pluck you from His hand?

---

6. Online: http://www.cyberhymnal.org/htm/s/o/soldiers.htm

Believe that Jesus reigns, all power in Him is giv'n:
Believe, till freed from sin's remains; believe yourselves in Heav'n.

7. To keep your armor bright, attend with constant care,
    Still walking in your Captain's sight, and watching unto prayer.
    Ready for all alarms, steadfastly set your face,
    And always exercise your arms, and use your every grace.

8. Pray without ceasing, pray, your Captain gives the word;
    His summons cheerfully obey and call upon the Lord;
    To God your every want in instant prayer display,
    Pray always; pray and never faint; pray, without ceasing, pray!

9. In fellowship alone, to God with faith draw near;
    Approach His courts, besiege His throne with all the powers of prayer:
    Go to His temple, go, nor from His altar move;
    Let every house His worship know, and every heart His love.

10. To God your spirits dart, your souls in words declare,
    Or groan, to Him Who reads the heart, the unutterable prayer:
    His mercy now implore, and show forth His praise,
    In shouts, or silent awe, adore His miracles of grace.

11. Pour out your souls to God, and bow them with your knees,
    And spread your hearts and hands abroad, and pray for Zion's peace;
    Your guides and brethren bear for ever on your mind;
    Extend the arms of mighty prayer, ingrasping all mankind.

12. From strength to strength go on, wrestle and fight and pray,
    Tread all the powers of darkness down and win the well fought day.
    Still let the Spirit cry in all His soldiers, "Come!"
    Till Christ the Lord descends from high and takes the conquerors home.

Addendum B

Stand Up, Stand Up for Jesus

GEORGE DUFFIELD'S SIX VERSES[7]

1. Stand up!—stand up for Jesus, Ye soldiers of the cross!
   Lift high His royal banner, It must not suffer loss.
   From victory unto victory His army shall He lead
   Till every foe is vanquished and Christ is Lord indeed.

2. Stand up!—stand up for Jesus! The solemn watchword hear;
   If, while ye sleep He suffers, away with shame and fear!
   Where'er ye meet with evil, Within you or without,
   Charge for the God of Battles, and put the foe to rout.

3. Stand up!—stand up for Jesus! The trumpet call obey;
   Forth to the mighty conflict In this His glorious day!
   Ye that are men, now serve Him against unnumbered foes;
   Let courage rise with danger And strength to strength oppose.

4. Stand up!—stand up for Jesus! Stand in His strength alone;
   The arm of flesh will fail you, Ye dare not trust your own.
   Put on the Gospel armor, Each piece put on with prayer;
   Where duty calls or danger, Be never wanting there.

5. Stand up!—stand up for Jesus! Each soldier to his post;
   Close up the broken column And shout through all the host:
   Make good the loss so heavy In those that still remain
   And prove to all around you That death itself is gain.

6. Stand up!—stand up for Jesus! The strife will not be long;
   This day the noise of battle, The next, the victor's song.
   To him that overcometh A crown of life shall be;
   He with the King of Glory shall reign eternally.

---

7. Polack, *The Handbook to the Lutheran Hymnal*, 319–20.

Addendum C

Am I a Soldier of the Cross?

ISAAC WATTS' SIX VERSES[8]

1. Am I a soldier of the cross, a follower of the lamb?
    And shall I fear to own His cause or blush to speak His name?

2. Must I be carried to the skies on flowery beds of ease?
    While others fought to win the prize, and sailed through bloody seas?

3. Are there no foes for me to face? Must I not stem the flood?
    Is this vile world a friend to grace, to help me on to God?

4. Sure I must fight, if I would reign, increase my courage, Lord!
    I'll bear the toil, endure the pain, Supported by Thy word.

5. Thy saints, in all this glorious war, shall conquer, though they die;
    They view the triumph from afar, and seize it with their eye.

6. When that illustrious day shall rise, and all Thy armies shine
    In robes of victory through the skies, the glory shall be Thine.

---

8. Wells, *A Treasure of Hymns*, 1914.

11

What's with Our Christmas Carols?

CHRISTMAS CAROLS CONSTITUTE THE music most likely to have been memorized by hosts of people, believers and nonbelievers alike. Innumerable families have "grandmother's book of carols" sitting on a shelf somewhere around the house. No one escapes this music as it is played in every store and on every street during the months of November and December. Almost everyone has been caroling or been serenaded by carolers, and quite often these singers are singing from memory. During the Christmas season, however, those attending one of our mainline churches must be prepared to sing many of these carols from the hymnal, since to depend upon memory is to risk embarrassment. And this could occur during the singing of what is most likely the most popular Christmas carol in the world, *Silent night! Holy night!*

An autographed manuscript of the carol, only discovered in 1995 and now in the collection of the Oberndorf Silent Night Museum, reveals that it was written by the Rev. Josef Mohr (1792–1848) in 1816. On Christmas Eve, 1818, Mohr, then assistant priest of the St. Nicholas Church in Oberndorf, Austria, asked the acting organist, Franz Gruber (1787–1863), to set the text for their two voices, choir, and guitar. The resulting composition was sung that evening, with Mohr singing the tenor part, Gruber the bass, and the church choir the refrains of each verse, while Mohr accompanied on the guitar.[1] The carol spread rapidly and was received with acclaim almost immediately. Although a number of versions in English have appeared, its definitive translation into English was published in 1859 by John Freeman Young, who was in later years consecrated Bishop of the Episcopal Church of Florida.

---

1. Http://www.hymnsandcarolsofchristmas.com/Hymns_and_Carols/Notes_On_ Carols/silent_night, 2.

At the time of its composition, Gruber was schoolmaster and parish organist in the nearby town of Arnsdorf. In 1897, a memorial tablet was placed on the schoolhouse there with this inscription:

> Silent night! Holy night!
> Who composed thee, hymn divine?
> Mohr it was who wrote each line,
> Gruber found my tune sublime.—
> Teacher together with priest.[2]

Perhaps its most famous performance was when it was sung simultaneously in English and German by troops during the Christmas truce of 1914 at Ypres, Belgium. Soldiers defied their officers by exchanging gifts, sometimes addresses, and drank together in the "No Man's Land" between their trenches. In 1999, a cross was erected near Ypres to commemorate the occasion, with the inscription:

> *1914*
> *The Khaki Chum's Christmas Truce*
> *1999*
> *85 Years*
>
> *Lest We Forget.*[3]

This stands as one of the great testimonials to the power of the Christian faith to overcome hatred and of song to provide the bridge between antagonists.

As it is sung today, all versions agree for two verses, so every singer can feel comfortable. The UCC hymnal makes three changes in the third verse, however. While all others sing,

> Silent night! Holy night!
> Son of God, love's pure Light
> Radiant beams from Thy holy face,
> With the dawn of redeeming grace.

The New Century Hymnal introduces this gratuitous change in the second line:

> Child of God, love's pure light.

---

2. Polack, *The Handbook to the Lutheran Hymnal*, 460.
3. Http://en.wikipedia.org/wiki/Christmas_truce, 1.

as if there was ever a question about whether Jesus was a "son." It may very well be that, because the phrases "Son of God" and "Son of Man" are often juxtaposed in theological discussion about the nature of Christ, some may raise a question whenever the first phrase appears by itself. To consider this appearance of the phrase as patriarchal language strikes me as gratuitous, however, and I would suggest that to eliminate it here is simply uncalled for.

The second change made in the UCC hymnal is far more felicitous, as it renders the last two lines:

> Radiant beams from Thy holy face
> Bring the dawn of redeeming grace.

In my opinion, this change actually strengthens the carol, leading as it does into the refrain for the verse:

> Jesus, Lord, at Thy birth,
> Jesus, Lord, at Thy birth.

a refrain changed in the UCC hymnal to:

> Jesus Christ at your birth,
> Jesus Christ at your birth.

With such a change, this hymnal adheres to its stated policy of eliminating words like "Lord" from the language of the hymns, successfully accomplished in 125 of the 152 hymns that used the word in their original composition. The policy also called for changing archaic terms like the second person singular "thy" and "thine" to "you" and "yours." One may quibble over the latter, but the refusal to recognize Jesus as "Lord" strikes at the very basis of the faith.

Writing to the church in Corinth, the Apostle Paul said,

> . . . no one can say "Jesus is Lord" except by the Holy Spirit,
> (NRSV, I Corinthians 12: 3)

and later, in his letter to the Romans, he wrote:

> But what does it say? "The word is near you, on your lips and in your heart" (that is, the word of faith that we proclaim); because if you confess with your lips that Jesus is Lord and believe in your heart that God raised him from the dead, you will be saved
> (NRSV, Romans 10:8-9)

The most primitive Christian profession of faith thus appears to have been "Jesus is Lord." Nor is that all.

In the Greek translation of the Old Testament, the Septuagint (LXX), the word chosen for the unpronounceable name of God, that is, the four-letter tetragrammaton YHWH [יהוה], was the Greek word for "Lord" [ὁ κύριος = ho kurios]. In the first century CE, as the primitive Christian movement spread into the Greek-speaking Jewish Diaspora of the Mediterranean world, its profession of "Jesus is Lord" spoke loudly and clearly to all readers of the LXX. On the basis of this profession, the church has spread across the globe in the millennia since. To now decide that such a profession of faith is either patriarchal, sexist, or both, and must therefore be excised strikes me as doubly problematical, being both unacceptable theology and indescribable arrogance.

One other difference met in the hymnals has nothing to do with gender-inclusive language, but rather involves a fourth verse sung by Baptists, Methodists, and Presbyterians. This verse apparently comes from an anonymous translator, not having been the work of John F. Young, and would appear to be an alternative rendering of the last German stanza. It is thus omitted by Episcopalians, Lutherans, and the UCC. If, however, this most popular Christmas carol has survived virtually intact in recent hymnody, the same cannot be said about another well-known carol.

God Rest You Merry, Gentlemen was called "the most popular of Christmas carols" by A. H. Bullen in his 1885 book, *Carols and Poems*.[4] It existed in two versions, one with seven verses and the other with eight. "God rest you merry" means "God keep you merry," but the comma after "merry" is often left out, thus inaccurately making the carol seem to sing about "merry gentlemen." The tune is that to which the carol was sung in the streets of London in the latter nineteenth century.[5] In spite of its one-time popularity, however, this carol has disappeared from all hymnals save that of the Episcopalians. Yet a look at its words makes one wonder why, as it has very few offensively gender-specific words, and these can be changed easily without disturbing the sense of the carol, as can be seen in what follows.

The Episcopalian hymnal prints four verses of the carol, presenting the first verse in this manner:

4. Dearmer, *The Oxford Book of Carols*, 25.
5. ibid.

> God rest you merry, gentlemen, let nothing you dismay;
> remember Christ our Savior was born on Christmas Day,
> to save us all from Satan's power when we were gone astray.

with the refrain of,

> O tidings of comfort and joy, comfort and joy;
> O tidings of comfort and joy.

The word "gentlemen" is the only possible term in this verse that might give offense gender-wise, and one could easily render it as "gentlefolk," "Christian-folk," or something similar, as has been done with *Good Christian Men, Rejoice,* successfully "sanitized" to *Good Christian Friends, Rejoice*. Otherwise this verse compresses the gospel of the Incarnation into a few marvelous lines that emphasize the joy of Christian life, the birth of Christ our Savior, his victory over the powers of evil, and the reality of our sin. In other words, this is a "jam-packed" theological statement.

For its second verse, the carol has:

> From God our heavenly Father a blessed angel came
> and unto certain shepherds brought tidings of the same:
> how that in Bethlehem was born the Son of God by name.

plus Refrain. Here we are given the chance to sing the message of the Gospel of Luke 2:1–20, with its story of the worshiping shepherds. To the extent that language about God as "our heavenly Father" and Jesus as the "Son of God" is considered patriarchal and therefore offensive, then this verse is packed with gender-offensive phrases. On the other hand, since believers are enjoined by Jesus in the Lord's Prayer itself to refer to God as "our Father in heaven," and Jesus himself is called the "Son of God" throughout most of the New Testament, it is difficult to sympathize with those who find these phrases nothing more than examples of male-domineering language that must be eliminated from the theological lexicon and the vocabulary of song. One might ask whether such agitation is too much of a protest, since to identify these phrases in this carol as concerned with gender specification is tunnel vision, pure and simple.

The words of the third verse continue the story:

> "Fear not, then," said the angel, "Let nothing you afright,
> this day is born a Savior of a pure virgin bright,

to free all those who trust in him from Satan's power and might."

plus Refrain. There would appear to be nothing here to invite concern about gender-inclusive language, and consequently nothing to require omission.

The same cannot be said about the fourth verse, although the Episcopalian hymnal seems to solve the problem:

> Now to the Lord sing praises, all you within this place,
> and with true love and brotherhood each other now embrace;
> this holy tide of Christmas all others doth deface.

plus Refrain. To create a gender-neutral second line, the Episcopalians now have:

> and with true love and charity each other now embrace;

a gender-inclusive rephrasing that catches the meaning quite well.

All of which is to say that Baptists, Lutherans, Methodists, Presbyterians, and the UCC have overreacted to a single word in the title of this carol. What was once "the most popular Christmas carol" deserves to continue in the repertoire for this reason alone, if for no other. If a change or two are required to make its language sufficiently gender neutral for the contemporary world, this can be done easily. By refusing to make such changes and include this song in their hymnals, the goal of those concerned about gender-inclusive language is actually defeated, since most church members will continue to sing the older, gender-offensive words as they enjoy what continues to be one of the more popular and easy-to-sing Christmas carols.

While *God Rest Ye Merry* has been ignored by our contemporary hymnals, the same cannot be said for the popular *Angels, from the Realms of Glory*, as it is included by all. When this is said, however, it must also be noted that not a verse is left unscathed, although only some of the changes affect the meaning. Written by James Montgomery (1771–1854), it was first published in the December 24, 1816, edition of the *Sheffield Iris*, a newspaper he had established in 1794.[6] Of him it was said, "His ear for rhythm was exceedingly accurate and refined. His knowledge of Holy Scripture was most extensive. His religious views

---

6. ibid., 241.

were broad and charitable. His devotional spirit was of the holiest type."[7] He was imprisoned twice, in 1795 and again in 1796, for political articles for which he was held responsible.

The two most significant changes to the carol are the different words used for the refrain in *The New Century Hymnal* and the new fourth stanza found in the hymnals of both Presbyterians and Lutherans. The former reflects concerns about gender, while the latter is a paean to the Trinity. These will be discussed in connection with the verses where they first appear.

The first verse is still generally sung as Montgomery wrote it:

> Angels, from the realms of glory,
> Wing your flight o'er all the earth;
> Ye who sang creation's story
> Now proclaim Messiah's birth:
> Come and worship, come and worship,
> Worship Christ the new-born king!

Only the Lutherans and the UCC worry about the archaic "Ye," the first changing it to "Once you sang" and the second to "As you sang." But neither of these has any gender significance.

The UCC alteration of the refrain, however, does reflect concerns about gender, as it reads:

> Come and worship, come and worship,
> Worship Christ, give thanks and sing.

Here the title of "King" denied to Christ, just as it was by the UCC hymnal in its treatment of the second line of the refrain of *The First Nowell*, where,

> born is the King of Israel,

has become,

> born in a manger, Emmanuel.

Once again we see the title of "King" denied to Christ, as such language is both too hierarchical and too sexist: on the one hand it smacks of domination and on the other its masculinity is balanceable by the

---

7. Julian, *A Dictionary of Hymnology*, 764. Dearmer, *Songs of Praise Discussed*, 47: "Montgomery was once asked by a Whitby solicitor, 'Which do you think of your poems will live?' and he answered, 'None, Sir, nothing except perhaps a few of my hymns.'"

feminine "Queen." Thus is a redefinition required as the historic role of Christ as Prophet, Priest, and King is shredded. Once again, then, just as it did with the word "Lord" in its treatment of *Silent Night*, the UCC hymnal eliminates language that suggests Christ is due obedience on the part of the believer. And these altered refrains are what *The New Century Hymnal* appends to every verse.

The second verse has, in its third line, an expression that many would think requires a change:

> Shepherds in the field abiding,
> Watching o'er your flocks by night,
> God with man is now residing;
> Yonder shines the infant Light:

Only the Baptists retain this wording, with all others but the Episcopalians singing,

> God with us is now residing.

Instead of the first person plural, Episcopalians are now singing,

> God with you is now residing.

It might be interesting to ask to whom this second person pronoun refers, if not to the singers.

The third verse has but one change, as the Baptists and the UCC eliminate the third person singular masculine pronoun in the fourth line:

> Sages, leave your contemplations;
> Brighter visions beam afar;
> Seek the great Desire of nations;
> Ye have seen His natal star:

The Baptists change both the pronoun and the seldom-used word "natal" by singing,

> You have seen the Infant's star,

while the UCC change the line to:

> guided by Christ's natal star.

What's with Our Christmas Carols?

The final verse is the challenging one for all those who have memorized this carol, as three hymnals have made significant changes. Montgomery wrote:

> Saints before the altar bending,
> Watching long in hope and fear,
> Suddenly the Lord, descending,
> In His temple shall appear:

While preserving this verse, *The New Century Hymnal* changes the last two lines in keeping with its customary practice of eliminating the word "Lord:"

> Suddenly, your prayers attending,
> Christ beside you shall appear.

By this change, the UCC shifts the scene from the first century with Simeon, Anna, the Jerusalem Temple and the appearance of Jesus, to the present day and the presence of Christ with the believer today.

Meanwhile, the Lutherans and Presbyterians have created a new fourth and final verse having no relation to Montgomery's words other than the refrain:

> All creation, join in praising
> God the Father, Spirit, Son,
> Evermore your voices raising
> To the eternal Three in One:

While this is a glorious and welcome affirmation of Trinitarian theology, it will surely present a challenge to carolers versed in Montgomery's words. At least, however, these two hymnals have agreed on the wording for the new stanza.

This discussion of concerns about our Christmas carols should not conclude without mention of *Joy to the World*, especially since *The New Century Hymnal* deserts its customary practice in its treatment of the word "Lord." The first line of the carol as found in all hymnals is,

> Joy to the world! The Lord is come.

Remarkably, this is left standing in the UCC hymnal, although the following note is placed at the bottom of the page:

> *Stanza 1 may be sung,* "Joy to the world! The Sovereign comes"

This exception to its usual practice by the editors of this hymnal should not be ignored, however.

This is especially true in light of changes made in the second line, where most follow Isaac Watts' original:

> Let earth receive her King.

Lutherans simply eliminate the reference to the femininity of "earth" by changing "her" to "its," a rather simple effort to eliminate language of gender. The UCC, however, rewrites the line in this manner:

> Let earth its praises bring.

Not only is earth as feminine eliminated, but the word "King" has also disappeared. In other words, the UCC may have allowed "Lord" to remain, but it would not permit both "Lord" and "King" to stand in the same verse. The third line enjoins "every heart prepare Him room," sung by all but the UCC, whose hymnal changes this to, "prepare Christ room," an understandable substitution.

The only problem encountered in the second verse occurs in line two, where only the Baptists follow Watts,

> Let men their songs employ.

Episcopalians and Presbyterians make the change to,

> Let us their songs employ,

while Lutherans, Methodists, and the UCC sing,

> Let all their songs employ.

Fortunately for today's singer, this is such a small difference that the person singing the original from memory will probably not even notice the change.

Verse three, with its graphic depiction of a sinful world, thorn-infested ground, and cursed situation overwhelmed by the blessings of Christ, is omitted by the UCC, while this is the only hymnal to change the gender-specific language in verse four:

> He rules the world with truth and grace,
> And makes the nations prove
> the glories of His righteousness,
> And wonders of His love. *[refrain]*

The New Century Hymnal begins the verse, "Christ rules" and elsewhere changes "His" to "God's," thereby shifting the meaning somewhat from an emphasis upon the righteousness and love of Christ to that of God, in the process inviting questions about the nature of the relationship between Christ and God. This confusion, however, as we discuss elsewhere, may be found often in the general tendency to simply replace the masculine personal pronoun with "God."

The Oxford Book of Carols includes almost two hundred songs and, although only a handful have been addressed in this chapter, we can see both the verbal uncertainty and the theological confusion found in the contemporary versions of our Christmas carols. As is the case with our hymns in general, it is no longer possible to feel comfortable singing the carols from memory, as every church has meandered on its own to make gender-inclusive changes. In addition, *The New Century Hymnal* in particular has introduced changes that seem to strike at the very roots of the faith, to the probable surprise of its UCC membership.

Addendum

Stille Nacht and Silent Night[8]

1. Stille Nacht! Heilige Nacht!	**1. Silent night! Holy night!**
Alles scläft; einsam wacht	All's asleep, one sole light,
Nur das traute heilige Paar.	Just the faithful and holy pair,
Holder Knab im lockigten Haar,	Lovely boy-child with curly hair,
Schlafe in himmlischer Ruh!	Sleep in heavenly peace!
Schlafe in himmlischer Ruh!	Sleep in heavenly peace!
2. Stille Nacht! Heilige Nacht!	**2. Silent night! Holy night!**
Gottes Sohn! O wie lacht	God's Son laughs, O how bright.
Lieb' aus dienem göttlichen Mund,	Love from your holy lips shines clear,
Da uns schlägt die rettende Stund',	As the dawn of salvation draws near,
Jesus in deiner Geburt!	Jesus, Lord, with your birth!
Jesus in deiner Geburt!	Jesus, Lord, with your birth!
3. Stille Nacht! Heilige Nacht!	**3. Silent night! Holy night!**
Die der Welt Heil gebracht,	Brought the world peace tonight,
Aus des Himmels goldenen Höhn	From the heaven's golden height
Uns der Gnaden Fülle lässt seh'n	Shows the grace of His holy might
Jesum in Menschendestalt	Jesus, as man on this earth!
Jesum in Menschendestalt	Jesus, as man on this earth!
4. Stille Nacht! Heilige Nacht!	**4. Silent night! Holy night!**
Wo sich heut' alle Macht	Where today all the might
Väterlicher Liebe ergoss	Of His fatherly love us graced
Und als Bruder huldvoll um-schloss	And then Jesus, as brother embraced.
Jesus die Völker der Welt,	All the peoples on earth!
Jesus die Völker der Welt,	All the peoples on earth!
5. Stille Nacht! Heilige Nacht!	**5. Silent night! Holy night!**
Lange schon uns bedacht,	Long we hoped that He might,
Als der Herr vom Grimme befreit,	As our Lord, free us of wrath,
In der Väter urgrauer Zeit	Since times of our father He hath
Aller Welt Schonung verhiess,	Promised to spare all mankind!
Aller Welt Schonung verhiess,	Promised to spare all mankind!

8. JCRH, *The Hymnal 1940 Companion*, 27.

6. Stille Nacht! Heilige Nacht!	6. Silent night! Holy night!
Hirten erst kundgemacht	Shepherds first see the sight.
Durch der Engel Alleluja,	Told by angelic Alleluja,
Tönt es laut bei Ferne und Nah:	Sounding everywhere, both near and far:
Jesus der Retter ist da!	Christ the Savior is here!"
Jesus der Retter ist da!	Christ the Savior is here!"

12

Praise, My Soul, the King (God) of Heaven

AS WE HAVE SEEN, the patriarchal language of hierarchy and its theological expression in masculine terminology has been of considerable concern to our hymnal editors. It has led to a number of changes in the language of our hymns, of which we have examined only a few. These few, however, have given insight into the various words and ideas that have raised concern, as well as the different ways these concerns have been addressed. Helpfully, *The Presbyterian Hymnal* has printed one hymn with its alternative on the facing page, thereby allowing a comparative examination.

Praise, My Soul, the King of Heaven, Henry Francis Lyte's (1793–1847) paraphrase of Psalm 103, appeared in his *The Spirit of the Psalms*, published in 1834. With its constant refrain of "Praise Him!" one could almost think of it as the first praise song, although since our hymnals change this to "Alleluia," the similarity tends to disappear. Lyte was priest of All Saints' parish of Brixham, England, from 1824 till his death in 1847. This hymn by Lyte, set to the tune LAUDA ANIMA by John Goss (1800–1880) in 1869, was adapted for the Ecumenical Women's Center in 1974. While other hymnals change Lyte's words to create more inclusive language, *The Presbyterian Hymnal* prints the original (for the most part) as Hymn 478 with its adaptation across the page as Hymn 479. Surprisingly, *The New Century Hymnal* prints neither. In what follows, Lyte's original version and its alternative are printed side-by-side, with comments between each verse, including proposed changes in the various hymnals

Verse One

Lyte's Version	Alternate Version
Praise, my soul, the King of heaven;	Praise, my soul, the God of heaven,
To His feet thy tribute bring;	Glad of heart your carols raise;
Ransomed, healed, restored, forgiven,	Ransomed, healed, restored, forgiven,
Who like me His praise should sing?	Who, like me, should sing God's praise?
Alleluia! Alleluia!	Alleluia! Alleluia!
Praise the everlasting King.	Praise the Maker all your days!

"Ever since Miriam and Moses first sang their victory song on the dry side of the sea, God has been worshiped as the king of Israel and of the church (Exod 15:18)."[1] So wrote Kathryn L. Roberts, noting that king as metaphor of God permeates Scripture from the Pentateuch through Psalms and Prophets and into the New Testament Gospels, to culminate with the Lamb seated at the right hand of God in the heavenly throne room (Rev 22:3). God is thus presented as the comforter in life today, the assurance of justice in a depraved world, the victor over life's defeats, and the hope of the future.

The alternative changes both the words and the theological content of the hymn. The ostensibly offensive concept of kingship is replaced with a more egalitarian one where each self-governing person is drawn into relationship with God, thereby presenting a commonwealth more in line with our modern democratic principles. In this contemporary state, God is less demanding and more readily available as counselor and advisor, who as Creator has launched humankind on its journey of progress. Although this is a comforting image, it is diametrically opposed to the portrait the Bible describes of the relationship between God and humankind. In the words of a Director of Music under whose direction I sang for many years: "This choir is not a democracy!" Neither is the relationship between God and the church, God and humanity, or God and the world.

---

1. Roberts, "Our Eyes Will See the Beauty of the King: The Esthetics of Kingship," 117. The analysis of verse one follows Dr. Roberts' argument, and the reader is referred to her treatment for further study.

Some changes to Lyte's hymn are made by every hymnal. As already noted, all change his four-time repeated refrain of "Praise Him!" in line five to the twice-repeated "Alleluia! Alleluia!" while Baptists, Episcopalians, and Presbyterians change line four to,

> Evermore His praises sing.

To eliminate this masculine pronoun, Methodists change the fourth line to,

> Evermore God's praises sing,

already having changed line two to,

> to the throne thy tribute bring,

changes that have no effect on the meaning of the hymn. Interestingly, the alternative version renders the fourth line almost as Lyte originally wrote it,

> Who, like me, should sing God's praises?

The changes these hymnals make to verse one of the hymn as Lyte wrote it, then, have little effect on its theological content. The same, however, cannot be said for the alternative, which seems to substitute the commonwealth of the forgiven for the Kingdom of God. Such a substitution may not be readily apparent to the singer in worship, but by placing these versions in juxtaposition to one another, *The Presbyterian Hymnal* renders a great service by inviting one to study their differences. Such an examination yields considerable insight into the ideology of those implementing the plan to eliminate gender-specific language from our hymns.

Verse Two

Lyte's Version	Alternate Version
Praise Him for His grace and favor	Praise God for the grace and favor
To our fathers in distress;	Shown our forebears in distress;
Praise Him still the same forever,	God is still the same forever,
Slow to chide, and swift to bless:	Slow to chide, and swift to bless
Alleluia! Alleluia!	Alleluia! Alleluia!
Glorious in His faithfulness.	Sing our Maker's faithfulness.

In this second verse, the alternative hews fairly close to Lyte's original. "God" replaces "Him" and "forebears" replaces "fathers," while the third person affirmation about God is moved from line six to line three. In the original, the singer is urged to praise Him in line three, and God's faithfulness is affirmed in line six, while in the alternative, God's unchangeableness is affirmed in line three and the believer urged to sing in line six.

Only the Baptists continue to sing line two as Lyte wrote it, the Lutherans changing it almost to the alternative with,

> To our forebears in distress,

while the Presbyterians sing,

> To His people in distress.

Otherwise, the Baptist, Episcopalian, and Presbyterian hymnals are similar to Lyte's original, except in line three they all use "as ever" rather than "forever." It is not clear whether these editors meant to question the future or not, but by their change that is exactly what is done relative to God's changeless character. This pales in comparison, however, to the impact of the changes in the Methodist presentation.

The United Methodist Hymnal rewrites verse two as follows:

> Praise the Lord for grace and favor
> to all people in distress;
> Praise God, still the same as ever,
> Slow to chide, and swift to bless:
> Alleluia! Alleluia!
> Glorious now God's faithfulness.

Here not only have all gender-specific words been removed, but the hymn has also been changed to eliminate the possibility of what has been termed the "scandal of particularity." This refers to God's choice of Abraham and his family to be the vehicles of blessing:

> Now the Lord said to Abram, "Go from your country and your kindred and your father's house to the land that I will show you. I will make of you a great nation, and I will bless you, and make your name great, so that you will be a blessing. I will bless those who bless you, and the one who curses you I will curse; and in you all the families of the earth shall be blessed." (NRSV, Gen 12:1–3)

From this beginning, the Bible is replete with examples of the concept of election, first as it pertains to the Israelites, then to the Jews, and culminating in the New Testament with the Christian church. So the Methodists change "God's people" or "His people" to "all people," and any singularity that might pertain to the Christian confession or movement is removed. In its own way, this is as radical a change from Lyte's original as anything in the alternative version, suggesting as it does a universalism contrary to his thought, as well as to that of John Wesley, Methodism's founder. It has probably been a surprise to ordinary Methodist singers, too.

Verse Three

Lyte's Version	Alternate Version
Fatherlike He tends and spares us;	Like a loving parent caring,
Well our feeble frame He knows;	God knows well our feeble frame;
In His hands He gently bears us,	Gladly all our burdens bearing,
Rescues us from all our foes.	Still to countless years the same.
Alleluia! Alleluia!	Alleluia! Alleuia!
Widely as His mercy flows.	All within me, praise God's name!

The third verse begins with one of those gender-specific words that requires attention. In many ways, it evokes some of the same responses as does the word "king," in spite of the fact that Jesus enjoined his disciples when they prayed to begin, "Our Father in heaven." Even though all native speakers of English know that the term in this usage is a gender-less reference to God, many want to see it eliminated anyway. To that end, the alternative version makes the change to "loving parent." What follows, then, when linked with line four, significantly changes the content of the hymn, again.

The alternative version could have rendered line two as was done by the Methodists:

> well our feeble frame God knows,

which can then rhyme with the ending word "foes" of line four, or some other word as the Methodists did. This was not done, however. Instead of making this choice, the alternative version chose to say,

> God knows well our feeble frame,

thereby creating an ending that required a rewrite of line four, making it end with the word "same," which when done eliminated any reference to the "foes" in the original that might threaten the believer.

Furthermore, line three in the alternate is changed to make God the bearer of "all our burdens" rather than the one who "gently bears us" who need His constant support because of "our feeble frame." In other words, as in verse one, the alternative pictures humankind as standing upright. Though feeble, we humans welcome the God who bears all our burdens, particularly as we ourselves apparently do not need such support. The final line then lifts praise to "God's name," completing the -*ame* rhyming pattern of lines two, four, and six.

Interestingly, while the Baptists omit this entire verse, only the Lutherans felt it necessary to change its first word, as they made it,

> Tenderly he shields and spares us,

thereby assigning an adverb descriptive of fatherly care and eliminating the word itself. Furthermore, the Lutherans' final line agrees with Lyte, "Widely as" rather than the "Widely yet" of the rest. Otherwise, Episcopalians, Lutherans, and Presbyterians agree with Lyte elsewhere in this verse.

Again, the Methodists have created something new:

> Father-like, God tends and spares us;
> well our feeble frame God knows;
> mother-like, God gently bears us,
> Widely yet God's mercy flows.

While retaining "Father-like," the pronouns are replaced by the noun "God," so each of the four lines is plagued with the redundancy of the same repeated word. This, however, is such a common gender-neutral change in today's world that, boring as it is, its problematical grammar may be almost unnoticeable. Of far greater moment is the third line, beginning with "mother-like," thereby introducing a specifically feminine word to balance the masculinity of "father-like."

Whereas capital-F Father standing by itself is another word for God, capital-M Mother never is, and many might see the use of "mother-like" here by the Methodists to be a way of limiting "father-like" to nothing more than a masculine reference. To invite such a misunderstanding is to introduce ideas of gender into the Godhead that are in every way antithetical to sound theology, as the closest that Scripture comes to using language like this is in Isaiah 66:13,

> As a mother comforts her child, so I will comfort you; you shall be comforted in Jerusalem.

Here we have a simile used of an action by God that is described to be "like a mother," something far different from saying "God is mother." In contrast, as we have already noted, God is called "Father" in Scripture, and this repeatedly, especially in the New Testament. It bears repeating, however, that this is not nor is it intended to be gender suggestive.

The placing of "mother-like" into the text to balance "Father-like," well-meaning as it may have been, introduces a potential theological error of tragic dimensions into the rendering of this hymn. At the same time, the introduction of "mother-like" may have been a deliberate attempt to tamper with the gender of God, something that is definitely part of the agenda of some who approach God from psychology rather than biblically based theology. This has serious flaws, however. On the one hand, it is a misunderstanding to assign gender to God at all, since God is spirit rather than creature, and biological gender is meaningless outside of creature-hood. On the other hand, such tampering destroys the essential femininity of Israel and the church vis-à-vis God and Christ in the great number of marriage illustrations in both Old and New Testaments. Here the Methodists seem to have emulated the UCC practice whereby any reference to God as "Father" must also include God as "Mother" in the same hymn.

Verse Four

> Frail as summer's flower we flourish;
> Blows the wind and it is gone;
> But, while mortals rise and perish,
> God endures unchanging on:
> Praise Him! Praise Him! Praise Him! Praise Him!
> Praise the high eternal One.

Lyte's fourth verse is omitted by all save the Baptists, for whom it is the third verse, and has no parallel in the alternative version. Apparently, no one is willing to publish this hymn with more or less than four verses! Yet this verse, portraying the frailty of human kind, bridges the gap between verse three with its picture of God's supportive care of feeble humanity and the triumphant presentation of the heavenly-enthroned God worshiped by all creation. It is the choral rendition of the psalmist's words in Psalm 103:15–18:

> As for mortals, their days are like grass; they flourish like a flower of the field; for the wind passes over it, and it is gone, and its place knows it no more. But the steadfast love of the Lord is from everlasting to everlasting on those who fear him, and his righteousness to children's children, to those who keep his covenant and remember to do his commandments. (NRSV)

The contrast between the mortality of human life and the everlasting nature of God's love provides the hymn writer a means to call for praise of "the high eternal One."

The omission of this verse may provide some insight into contemporary church thought, where often the emphasis is more on the idea that "God accepts us where we are" than it is on "God has acted to save us." This last invites us to reflect on both from what and to what we have been saved, suggesting deficiencies in our natural lives together with the promise of a future led by the indwelling Spirit of the Lord. Furthermore, it allows consideration of the power of evil to wreck our lives as well as the world at large, an idea that we have already seen to be often avoided. In addition, that we have been saved by the action of a loving God rather than by any of our own acts suggests a hierarchical world out of our ultimate control. Ideas like these, however, are at odds with our post-modern, democratic, individualistic world view, and apparently one of the consequences of this is that many require such thoughts be changed. It seems that the contemporary position is that hymn verses implying such a view should be omitted, as has been done in this case with Lyte's fourth verse.

Verse Five

Lyte's Version	Alternate Version
Angels, help us to adore Him:	Angels, teach us adoration,
Ye behold Him face to face;	You behold God face to face;
Sun and moon, bow down before Him,	Sun and moon and all creation,
Dwellers all in time and space.	Dwellers all in time and space.
Alleluia! Alleluia!	Alleluia! Alleluia!
Praise with us the God of grace.	Praise with us the God of grace.

Praise, My Soul, the King (God) of Heaven 133

The final verse in each version is a glorious acclamation of the glory of God, the One praised by every being in any time and everywhere. Yet even as the alternative version closely parallels the original, its first line strikes a difference reminiscent of what we have already seen in verses one and three. Whereas the help of the angels is required in Lyte's version for us to adore God, in the alternate we appear as pupils, ready and able to be taught adoration. In addition, the object of our adoration is not even named until the closing line.

Furthermore, line three in the alternate opens several doors better left closed. In its attempt to be gender neutral, it eliminates the verb depicting the obeisance of the sun and moon, thereby placing these words in apposition to "Angels," thus inviting speculation about the possible identification of angels with the stars. Such an injection of the possibility of astrology into the believing singer's thoughts is unfortunate in the extreme. In addition, as the change creates greater scientific accuracy by eliminating the idea of the sun and moon bowing down to God, it unnecessarily removes a piece of poetic license that surely has never been taken literally. And these problems seem to have been the result of the choice of "creation" as the word to rhyme with "adoration." It would have been better if neither of these words had found their way into the hymn at these places.

While Episcopalians and Lutherans follow Lyte's original, the other hymnals make changes, some of greater import than others. For instance, Presbyterians alone change the last line to,

> Praise us all the God of grace,

hardly worth a mention. On the other hand, Baptists make several changes having considerably greater impact, although none affect gender-specific language.

The Baptist Hymnal presents the first four lines of this verse as follows:

> Angels in the height adore Him;
> Ye behold Him face to face;
> Saints triumphant, bow before Him;
> Gathered in from every race.

With their first line, the Baptists accomplish several changes from Lyte's original. In the first place, angels are located "in the height" and the possibility of their working to help us believers in worship or adoration is eliminated. At the same time, we as believers are removed from the verse until our appearance in the final line's "Praise with us." In the third line, all reference to the created order is removed, as the saints are the ones bowing down in worship and not "sun and moon." By making this change, the extent of adoration is limited to sentient beings and the physical world is ignored, although Lyte's original was reminiscent of Paul's striking expression in Romans 8:22–23:

> We know that the whole creation has been groaning in labor pains until now; and not only the creation, but we ourselves, who have the first fruits of the Spirit, groan inwardly while we wait for adoption, the redemption of our bodies. (NRSV)

Having removed this idea, the fourth line is rewritten to emphasize the ecumenicity of the Church in its worldwide mission.

Nor are the Baptists alone in their changes. *The United Methodist Hymnal* parallels the Baptist but with gender concerns addressed as well:

> Angels in the heights adoring,
> you behold God face to face;
> Saints triumphant, now adoring,
> gathered in from every race.

The comments on the first two lines would be the same as those already made, with the additional note that the Methodists eliminate the pronoun, leaving the object of the angels' adoration to be supplied, and substituting "God" for "Him" in the second line. This has then reduced the Methodists to repeating the word "adoring" in line three to rhyme with itself in the first line, while all others have, "bow before Him." With these additional observations, the remarks about the Methodist treatment of this verse replicate those made about the Baptist rendition.

This examination of the hymn, *Praise, My Soul, the King of Heaven*, as it has been edited by contemporary hymnals and adapted in 1974 for the Ecumenical Women's Center has revealed several contemporary concerns. The desire to eliminate gender-specific language is evident, although some hymnals are more rigorous than others in this effort. Beyond this, however, often there seems to be a clear unwillingness to recognize a hierarchical structure between believers and the Almighty, as if somehow the Church is a democratic assembly that has elected God to chair its activities. In addition, there appears to be a genuine reluctance to admit the existence of evil with power to threaten believers. Finally, in some attempts to be gender inclusive, there is an implication of sexual identification within the Godhead.

13

Conclusion

OUR RELIGIOUS LANGUAGE DETERMINES how we decode our spiritual life. Ideally, our Holy Scripture provides the language by which we talk about the Divine and the hymns of the faith reflect how we think and feel about our religious beliefs. Discontinuity between the language of their beliefs and that of Bible, songs, and/or worship liturgies invites a general feeling of frustration on the part of church members. Discontinuities of this sort as a result of concerns about gender-neutral language have been the topic of the preceding chapters of this book. Gender neutrality is important to practice in both Bible translations and hymns as a part of the attempt to ensure that our religious language reflects our culture as much as possible. This effort, however, is being misused to advance a different ideology altogether.

Our first Authorized Version of Scripture, the great English translation known as the King James Version of 1611, together with the writings of William Shakespeare created modern English, but we would not want to read either as they were first composed. Gender inclusiveness is one of the important elements of contemporary language, and as we have noted, the editors of the *New Revised Standard Version* [NRSV], our latest Authorized Version, per their instructions worked to achieve gender neutrality. To that end, they made a distinction between the language about the Divine and that about human beings.

For the most part, the translation reflects the way the original Hebrew, Aramaic, and Greek languages talked about God. It is a modern ideology that makes generic "he" unacceptable even though it is intelligible, an ideology rejected by the NRSV in its language about God. This has meant that at almost every turn, where "he," "his," or "him" has been used to refer to the Lord, the NRSV has unabashedly retained the pronoun. Although in a few places its attempt to remove such language has led to some confusion, in general such changes have been avoided. Yet the liturgies of many of the mainline churches as well as others that have adopted the NRSV, using it for study as well as for public worship, have failed to follow the lead of this version of Holy Scripture in their language about God. The following Call to Worship illustrates the problem:

> Leader: People of God, we do not live by our own strength alone, but draw life from God.
> People: God is our root, deeply planted and firmly established.
> Leader: God anchors all life, and without God there is no life.
> People: Let us draw close to God, listening for guidance and trusting in divine love.
> All: Let us worship God together.[1]

The word "God" is used seven times in this five-statement responsive litany, where there is additionally one synonym, "divine love," used instead of "God's love," which last would have made for eight uses of the same word.

As is plain to see, the liturgy requires a personal pronoun, if for no other reason than good grammar. Beyond that, the word "God" is not descriptive in a personal sense and cannot add to our understanding of the potential for a relationship between the Divine and an individual human person. In such attempts to avoid the masculine pronoun, the liturgies of these Bible-based churches ignore the language of their Bible about God, making it appear as if believers come only from the theologically uneducated and the linguistically deficient.

The God language of the NRSV with its pronouns presents an open invitation to the reader and hearer for a personal relationship. The God language of the liturgy just cited is formal and structured, inviting the reader and hearer to draw close but not to touch. From it, we learn that God gives us life, that He grounds us, that He anchors all life, and that if we will draw close and trust Him, He will guide us. Lacking the personal pronoun, however, nothing in the liturgy suggests the possibility of a personal relationship with this God. With the disappearance of personal language for use in talking about God, the worshiping believer is suddenly faced with the impossible task of being invited to think about God in personal terms but without the language to do so. In light of such confusion, it is no wonder that believers, frustrated and wondering why

1. August 16, 2009, bulletin of a church I leave unidentified.

they feel betrayed, are leaving the mainline churches to search elsewhere for spiritual sustenance.

Most members of our mainline churches are native speakers of English. They both read and listen to the Scriptures in the English language, hearing as they do how one is to talk about God. When liturgies like that presented earlier appear in worship, these same members recognize that something is not right. They may not identify the problem, but they know that English is not spoken that way. In other words, they feel deep down that they are in the presence of something phony. When what is under consideration is the complete commitment of the believer's life in faith to Jesus, then talking in a way that suggests a counterfeit will immediately halt any further movement. No one bets her or his life on something suspected of being a fake.

Unfortunately, in its attempt to address gender-specific language about people, the NRSV compounds the problem of personal language identified earlier. Many of the Psalms, for instance, are intensely personal in nature. By substituting the plural for so many of the appearances of the masculine singular, God appears to relate to the group rather than to the individual. Instead of augmenting an experience with God's Word, then, the change from the singular to the plural serves to separate a reader and hearer from the Word of God. This may help explain why the NRSV has not attained the popularity of previous Authorized Versions or of some of the other modern translations.

At the same time as language is eliminated that supports a personal relationship between God and the individual believer, the language emphasizing the solidarity of believers with one another also is eliminated. We have considered how the treatment of both "Adam" and "brothers" has often failed in this regard. In the case of the former, in places the entire human species is embodied in the single term, "man," and to avoid its use is to miss a crucial point. As for the latter term, whole subjects like adoption, the communion of saints, and the unity of the church fall by the wayside, thereby depriving members of critical doctrines of the faith.

At this point, it may be worth noting that the meaning of a word cannot be established separate from its context. English is replete with words that have multiple meanings, and one can find hundreds of examples by entering the words "polysemy" or "homograph" in an Internet search engine. For instance, although the word "fine" can mean excellent, or thin, or financial punishment, plus a number of technical meanings, no native speaker would misunderstand it in a sentence. In certain cases, the charge of illegitimate gender specificity results from the refusal to admit this fact.

The English-language reader used to be conditioned to interpret masculine pronouns, and such words as "man" and "mankind," in a manner that would use context to determine whether to decode them in a gender-inclusive or gender-specific way. Our problem today is that many would argue this is no longer the case. Yet even when a generally approved alternative, huMAN, is used, or any of its derivatives, one does not escape these three letters. In the same vein, perSON likewise fails to escape a similar three-letter masculine word. To a certain extent, some of the identifications of linguistic expressions as sexist and therefore requiring change result from deliberate obtuseness. Gender neutrality should require us to function at a far more sophisticated level than this sort of "zero-tolerance" to particular words that seem to be deliberately defined wrongly.

But back to our discussion of the NRSV. In the case of translations of the Bible, we should remember that there is a relationship between the Old and New Testaments, inasmuch as the writers of the latter assumed the former as their canon of Holy Scripture. Our translations should not blur this distinction, as happens in several places in the NRSV, where it looks as if the translators of the respective Testaments were working alone rather than in consort with one another. As it is, it is difficult enough to understand the New Testament as it relates to the Old without our translations adding to the problem.

In addition, we must always avoid allowing our concerns about gender to lead us into a distortion of the meaning of a passage, especially as sometimes a serious misunderstanding can come from a failure to recognize that the text presupposes a male audience.[2] For instance, in Matthew 5:31–32, Jesus' warning against frivolous divorce is framed entirely from the standpoint of the man:

---

2. When people are numbered in the Bible, it is the men who are numbered: Matthew 14:21, 15:38; Acts 4:4; Revelation 14:4. There are also statements that are unacceptable in today's climate, like "silly women" in I Timothy 3:6; "typical of old women" in 2 Timothy 4:7; "become like old women and tremble with fear" in Isaiah 19:16 (also Jeremiah 50:37, 51:30, and Nahum 3:13); and "stand firm and act like men" in I Corinthians 16:13, where all reflect how a man speaks to men.

... anyone who divorces his wife, except on the ground of sexual immorality, makes her commit adultery. (NRSV)

Here the hapless wife, who is innocent of any wrongdoing, is said to be *adulterated* by any remarriage, yet in ancient times a woman had to remarry if she was to have any security. Jesus did not intend for anyone to draw from this saying any rule for the divorced woman, because the saying was *not meant to be read from the standpoint of the woman.* The woman is not even considered to be a morally responsible agent in it. The teaching is directed solely *at the divorcer.*

When all this is said, however, I would argue that the NRSV remains a useful version of Scripture because of its relatively careful use of notes. Almost every reservation expressed so far about a change made to achieve gender neutrality is identifiable within the NRSV by a note identifying the text of the original for the reader. The editors deserve our praise for taking such care, as well as our criticism for those places where changes were made without any note to indicate what has been done. Whether it is an improvement on the *Revised Standard Version* (RSV), its predecessor, I would suggest is questionable, however. Certainly, I continue to use the RSV for most purposes in preference to the NRSV.

As far as hymns are concerned, we need to remember that the faith as practiced is often the faith as sung. Hymns are a form of poetry and poetic license can be used to avoid non-inclusive language. Denominations need to get together and agree on their hymn changes, therefore, especially those denominations that work together in the World Council and National Council of Churches (the latter of which authorized the NRSV).

I grew up in years when the denominations were in serious conflict with one another, yet my friends and I always enjoyed group opportunities to sing, as all of us knew the same words to the same hymns. I find it ironic that what we now sing is sometimes different, even though the denominations are all heavily involved with one another, working together and talking union under the influence of the ecumenical movement. It is both sad and humorous to watch interdenominational groups sing *Joyful, Joyful, We Adore Thee,* for example, since many have memorized both words and tune to this very popular and meaningful hymn, but now find themselves confused as they try to sing it with others. It appears as if what we sing is slowly going its own way, denomination by denomination.

In all of this, today's hymnal editors follow the pattern established by their predecessors when they almost never annotate their changes. It is impossible to reconstruct a poet's original text from the words found in one of our contemporary hymnals. Of course, copyright issues have no currency, as many of our hymns are quite old. Nevertheless, all of us who know any poets or song writers are aware of the pride they take in their words and the time they spend laboring to find the exact phrase to express their sentiments. It is simply extreme arrogance to change these words without even a note to that effect. To be sure, there has not yet been developed an annotation system for this purpose, but I suspect little effort has been expended to do so, either. I think a challenge to future hymnal editors is called for to develop and implement a notation system that would protect the words of our authors.

Among the changes that have been made to the hymns of the church, those involving language about God are particularly distressing. In contrast to the practice of the editors of the NRSV, the hymnal editors have made a number of such changes. In the process, references to the "Fatherhood of God" tend to disappear in what might be recognized as a blatant attack on trinitarian language itself. It is as if the historical debates about the eternal Fatherhood and eternal Sonship of God never occurred.

It does, however, provide insight into the thinking of those that succeeded in obtaining the 2006 approval of the Presbyterian General Assembly for its action, reported this way by the Associated Press:

> The divine Trinity— "Father, Son and Holy Spirit"—could also be known as "Mother, Child and Womb" or "Rock, Redeemer, Friend" at some Presbyterian Church (U.S.A.) services under an action Monday by the church's national assembly. Delegates to the meeting voted to "receive" a policy paper on gender-inclusive language for the Trinity, a step short of approving it. That means church officials can propose experimental liturgies with alternative phrasings for the Trinity, but congregations won't be required to use them.[3]

This action may have been slipped past department heads by adroit staffers who wanted their pet policy enunciated by an unsuspecting General Assembly, but it created considerable excitement at the time.

3. "Presbyterians Suggest Gender-Inclusive Language in Worship," FOXNews.com, Monday, June 19, 2006.

Furthermore, it reflects the nature of the attack being launched against the Trinity in the name of gender-inclusive language.

The attack seems to reflect commitment to a syllogism of the following sort:

> (A) Patriarchal language must be eliminated from the Christian faith.
> (B) The doctrine of the Trinity is expressed in patriarchal language.
> (C) Therefore, the language of the Trinity must be eliminated.

Such a conclusion, however, not only fails to mirror the faith of church members, but it also actually offends the vast majority. When singing favorite hymns that no longer include their former ringing affirmations of the triune God, members understandably feel betrayed.

Furthermore, some hymnals are moving to eliminate the word "Lord" entirely, even though this is the name of God in the Old Testament, and the profession "Jesus is Lord" is the most primitive of the Christian confessions. Accompanying this movement is the elimination of phrases like the "kingdom of God" and references to God as "King." Such terms are considered hierarchical, similar to the same patriarchal language already condemned, and therefore to be eliminated as well. Obedience to Christ, however, has always been a staple of the religious diet of church members, and to have it suggested that Jesus only rules at the discretion of his followers is shocking.

Even if the proclamation of the supremacy of Christ is an affront to the individualism so rampant in our culture, that does not invalidate the Gospel message. The members of our churches, knowing that the message of the faith often challenges them and their style of life, rightfully expect their hymns to reflect that position. They do not see themselves as people who want God in their lives but do not want to change their lifestyles. When sentiments that challenge their lifestyles are removed from the hymns, members of our mainline churches will seek elsewhere for worship services that still sing their faith.

Closely associated with the removal of hierarchical language is the apparent dissolution of a serious appreciation of the power of evil. This is clearly evident in the elimination of hymns and phrases of a warlike nature. Virtually all of these hymns use the language of war to describe the conflict between the forces of Christ and those of evil, between the church and sin. In them, sin is recognized as a threat of terminal dimensions, and the confrontation with it a matter of extreme concern. So threatening is this situation that the crucifixion of Jesus was required to rescue humankind from the power of evil. Yet this classical expression of the work of Christ is exactly what is being removed, it too being identified as a reflection of hierarchical thought unfit for today's world.

Mainline church members, then, who may be now, or have been in the past, overwhelmed by forces of evil outside their control now find little understanding of this in their hymns. Furthermore, in the conflict against sin the idea that the Christian may be called in the name of God to suffer, perhaps even to die, has simply disappeared. Changes made to many of the hymns have trivialized the idea of sin to the point that wounded members may no longer find comfort in their shallow words. To the extent that this is so, it becomes a betrayal of the grossest sort.

There can be no perfection in language, and there is no standard for it. That is different, however, from having no standards at all. The tasks set before the translators of Holy Scripture and the editors of our church hymnals are immense. Bible translators are called upon to render the Biblical text into the current language of our culture while maintaining the integrity of the original. Fortunately, we speakers of English have been blessed with Authorized Versions for four centuries that have met this challenge in a superior manner. The current Authorized Version, the NRSV, has a rightful place in this succession, even though some of us may think it to be not quite of the same caliber as its predecessors.

In the same manner, hymnal editors are charged to filter what their members like to sing and to identify new musical statements of the faith. I would suggest that the members of our churches have the right to insist that their respective church leaders require that this be done with due respect (1) to the language about God found in their preferred version of Holy Scripture, the NRSV, (2) to elements of good English style, (3) to the original lyrics of the hymns, and (4) to the practice of their respective denominations.

In the final analysis, an examination of the implementation of contemporary concerns about gender-specific language in the Bible and in the hymns of the Church leads to the inexorable conclusion that, rather than linguistic concerns, many of the changes are being driven by an ideology that rejects hierarchy and patriarchy in favor of democratic egalitarianism. In song and liturgy, by the removal of personal pronouns God is reconceived in depersonalized language. In much of Scripture, the deeply personal relationship between God and individuals is submerged into the plural. While on the one hand affirming their biblical orientation, some hymnals in many of their hymns reject biblical language about God as gender-less spirit by injecting femininity into the Godhead. In these same hymnals, the idea of the church as a body of souls saved from overwhelming evil has disappeared from many hymns. Instead, the church has become a company of people committed to doing good. Slight alterations of wording in the hymns suffice to bring them into line with current ideology, alterations that are not readily discernible to unsuspecting church members. The worthy concern to make the language of the church more gender inclusive has been distorted into a movement to seduce the church to abandon its historical faith.

Did or did God not reveal His name, character, person, purpose, and Son very specifically in His Word written, that is, the Bible? If not, is there a Christian faith at all?

Is God changing, in process, evolving, or is He the same, yesterday, today, and forever—Father, Son, and Holy Spirit, the Trinity who IS unchangeably, KNOWS unchangeably, and WILLS unchangeably?

Are we only people questing in semi-despair for an elusive sense and meaning in life or, even more, are we also redeemed sinners who have responded to God's love in faith to enjoy a personal relationship through Jesus Christ?

If believers are robbed of the language of their Christian faith and of the doctrines that are distinctly theirs, then the ministry of the Gospel can be crippled. What we believe determines how we behave, and wrong belief ultimately means a wrong life. Each local church is but one generation short of potential extinction. The church is under attack by adherents to an egalitarian ideology radically opposed to the biblical portrayal of God, adherents who are using the gender-inclusive language movement to advance their cause. In this effort, they are being unwittingly abetted by church leaders who, understandably, even laudably, desire to be inclusive, but having failed to recognize the danger, have simply acquiesced to changes of language that involve many more issues than the simple concern about gender neutrality.

Bibliography

Adler, Rachel. "Feminist Judaism: Past and Future." *Cross Currents* 51.04, Winter, 2002, 484–89.
Associated Press. "New Methodist Hymnal Is Shorn of Stereotypes." *The New York Times*, June 20, 1989.
Associated Press. "Presbyterians Suggest Gender-Inclusive Language in Worship." Online: FOXNews.com, Monday, June 19, 2006.
Baring-Gould, Sabine. *Onward, Christian Soldiers*. Online: http://songsandhymns.org/hymns/detail/onward-christian-soldiers
Benson, Louis F., ed. *The Hymnal*. Philadelphia: The Presbyterian Board of Publication and Sabbath-School Work, 1911.
Board of Publication, Lutheran Church in America. *Lutheran Book of Worship*. Minneapolis, MN: Augsburg, 1978.
Brown, Francis, S. R. Driver, and Charles A. Briggs. *A Hebrew and English Lexicon of the Old Testament*. Oxford: Clarendon, 1955.
Bucke, Emory Stevens, General Editor. *Companion to the Hymnal: a Handbook to the 1964 Methodist Hymnal*. Nashville: Abingdon, 1970.
Butcher, Geoffrey et al., editors. *The Hymnal 1982*. New York, NY: The Church Hymnal Corporation, 1985.
Calvin, John. *Commentary on the Book of Psalms*. Translated by the Rev. James Anderson. 1843–1845. 5 volumes. Reprint. Grand Rapids: Eerdmans, 1949.
Campbell, Antony F., and Mark A. O'Brien. *Sources of the Pentateuch: Texts, Introductions, Annotations*. Minneapolis: Fortress, 1993.
Carrier, Richard. *The Empty Tomb: Jesus Beyond the Grave*. Amherst, NY: Prometheus, 2005.
Charlesworth, James H. *The Old Testament Pseudepighrapha* (2 volumes). Garden City, NY: Doubleday, 1985.
Clyde, Arthur G., editor. *The New Century Hymnal*. Cleveland, OH: Pilgrim, 1995.
Collins, Ace. *Stories Behind the Hymns That Inspire America*. Grand Rapids: Zondervan, 2003.
Covert, William Chalmers, editor, and Calvin Weiss Laufer, associate editor. *Handbook to The Hymnal*. Philadelphia: Presbyterian Board of Christian Education, 1935.
Dalitz, Christoph. *Fairest Lord Jesus*. Version 1.0 (2008/11/23). No pages. Online: PDF File: http://music.dalitio.de/
Dearmer, Percy. *Songs of Praise Discussed*. New York: Oxford University Press, 1933.
Dearmer, Percy, R. Vaughan Williams, and Martin Shaw. *The Oxford Book of Carols*. London: Oxford University Press, 1928.
Eco, Umberto. *The Aesthetics of Thomas Aquinas*. Translated by Hugh Bredin. Cambridge, MA: Harvard University Press, 1988.
Forbis, Wesley L., editor. *The Baptist Hymnal*. Nashville, TN: Convention, 1991.

Hadas, Moses, and John McLean. *Euripedes: Ten Plays*. New York: Bantam, 1963.
Higgs, Liz Curtis. *Bad Girls of the Bible, and What We Can Learn from Them*. Colorado Springs, CO: Waterbrook, 1999.
Joint Commission on the Revision of the Hymnal. *The Hymnal 1940 Companion*. New York: The Church Pension Fund, 1949.
Jones, David Hugh, editor. *The Hymnbook*. Philadelphia, PA: John Ribble, 1955.
Josephus, *Jewish Antiquities*. Translated by H. St. John Thackeray (*The Loeb Classical Library*). Cambridge, MA: Harvard University Press, 1967.
Julian, John. *A Dictionary of Hymnology*. 2 volumes. New York: Dover, 1907.
Kilpatrick, James J. "Save 'The Marseillaise!' and 'The Star-Spangled Banner!'" Columbia, SC: *The State Newspaper*, unknown issue.
King James Bible as found in *The Interpreter's Bible*. Edited by George A. Buttrick. Nashville: Cokesbury, 1952.
Lafargue, M. "Orphica." In *Old Testament Pseudepigrapha* (2 volumes). Edited by James H. Charlesworth. *ii*, 800. Garden City, NY: Doubleday, 1985.
Landsberg, Max, and Newton Mann. "Praise to the Living God." No pages. Online: http://www.oremus.org/hymnal/p/p102.html
Lingle, Walter L., editor. *The Presbyterian Hymnal*. Richmond, VA: John Knox, 1927.
Lucarini, Dan. *Why I Left the Contemporary Christian Music Movement*. Webster, NY: Evangelical, 2002.
Maimonides, Moses. *Yigdal*. No pages. Online: http://en.wikipedia.org/wiki/Yigdal
McKim, LindaJo, editor. *The Presbyterian Hymnal*. Louisville, KY: Westminster John Knox, 1990.
McIntosh, Peggy. "White Privilege: Unpacking the Invisible Knapsack." *Working Paper 189*: "White Privilege and Male Privilege: A Personal Account of Coming to See Correspondences through Work in Women's Studies." Wellesley, MA: Wellesley College Center for Research on Women, 1988.
Moulton, J. H., W. F. Howard, and Nigel Turner. *A Grammar of New Testament Greek* (4 volumes). Edinburgh: T & T Clark, 1908–1976.
New King James Bible. Nashville: Thomas Nelson, 1982.
New Revised Standard Version Bible. Peabody, MA: Hendrikson, 2004.
Ostriker, Alicia Suskin. *The Nakedness of the Fathers: Biblical Visions and Revisions*. New Brunswick, NJ: Rutgers University Press, 1994.
Otto, Rudolf. *The Idea of the Holy*. Translated by John W. Harvey. 1923. New York: Oxford, Galaxy, 1958.
Penelope, Julia. *Speaking Freely: Unlearning the Lies of the Fathers' Tongues*. New York: Pergamon, 1990.
Plaskow, Judith, and Carol P. Christ, editors. *Weaving the Visions: New Patterns in Feminist Spirituality*. San Francisco: Harper and Row, 1989.
Polack, W. G. *The Handbook to the Lutheran Hymnal*, Second and Revised Edition. St. Louis, MO: Concordia, 1942.
Revised Standard Version Bible. In *The Oxford Annotated Bible*. Edited by Herbert G. May and Bruce M. Metzger. New York: Oxford, 1965.
Roberts, Kathryn L. "Our Eyes Will See the Beauty of the King: The Esthetics of Kingship." *Word & World* xix (1999) 117–24.
Schussler Fiorenza, Elisabeth. *In Memory of Her: A Feminist Theological Reconstruction of Christian Origins*. New York: Crossroads, 1992.

———. *Jesus; Miriam's Child, Sophia's Prophet: Critical Issues in Feminist Christology.* New York: Continuum, 1994.

Sorge, Sheldon. "Don't Mess With My Music." *Presbyterians Today* 95/10 (December, 2005) 12–17.

Strong, James. *The New Strong's Exhaustive Concordance of the Bible.* Nashville: Thomas Nelson, 1984.

Sydnor, James R., editor. *Hymnal for Christian Worship.* Richmond, VA: John Knox Press, 1940.

Talbott, Rick. "Imagining the Matthean Eunuch Community: Kyriarchy on the Chopping Block." *Journal of Feminist Studies in Religion* 22-01, January, 2006, 21–43.

Truss, Lynne. *Eats, Shoots & Leaves.* New York: Gotham, 2004.

van Dyke, Henry. *Thy Sea is Great, Our Boats are Small and Other Poems of Today.* New York, NY: Revell, 1922.

———. *Joyful, Joyful, We Adore Thee.* No pages. Online: http://www.joyfulministry.com/joyfult.htm

Wells, Amos R. *A Treasure of Hymns.* Boston: United Society of Christian Endeavor, 1914.

Wesley, Charles. *Soldiers of Christ, Arise.* No Page. Online: http://www.cyberhymnal.org.htm/s/o/soldiers.htm

Wink, Walter. *The Human Being: Jesus and the Enigma of the Son of Man.* Minneapolis: Fortress, 2002.

Wren, Brian. *What Language Shall I Borrow? God-Talk in Worship: A Male Response to Feminist Theology.* New York: Crossroad, 1993.

Young, Carlton R., editor. *The United Methodist Hymnal.* Nashville, TN: The United Methodist Publishing House, 1989.

Hymn Index

TITLES AND TUNES

A Mighty Fortress, 76
Alas! And Did My Savior Bleed, 95n
Am I A Soldier of the Cross?, 103, 109
Angels, from the Realms of Glory, 116–119

Beautiful Savior, 65–73

CRUSADER HYMN, 68, 73

DIADEMATA, 103
Fairest Lord Jesus, 11, 67–73

God of Grace and God of Glory, 1
God Rest You Merry, Gentlemen, 114–16
Good Christian Friends, Rejoice, 115
Good Christian Men, Rejoice, 115

Hallelujah Chorus, 6
His Fatherhood and Love, 77
Hymn to Joy, 75

Joy to the World, 119–21
Joyful, Joyful, We Adore Thee, xvi, 11, 67, 75–85, 139

LAUDA ANIMA, 125
LEONI, 88–90

Messiah, 9, 32–33

O Love Divine, That Stooped to Share 80
Ode to Joy, 75
Onward, Christian Soldiers, 99–101

Praise, My Soul, the God of Heaven, 125–134
Praise, My Soul, the King of Heaven, 11, 125–134
Praise to the Living God, 89

QUEBEC, 80

ST. GERTRUDE, 100
Schönster Herr Jesu, 74
SILVER STREET, 103
Soldiers of Christ, Arise, 102–3
Stand Up, Stand Up for Jesus, 101–2, 108
Silent Night! Holy Night!, 111–14, 118, 122–24
Stille Nacht, 122–24

The God of Abraham Praise, 11, 67, 87–99
The Son of God Goes Forth to War, 104–5
The Whole Armor of God, 102

We All Believe in One True God, 69

Scripture Index

OLD TESTAMENT

Genesis

1:1—2::4a	29
1:5	24
1:26-27	27-28
2:4b-25	29
2:7	27, 30
2:19-23	31
2:23b	30
2:24a	30
2:25a	30
2:25	31
3:28	59
4	53-54
5:24	19
15:6	16-17
19:17	16

Exodus

15:18	126
33:19—34:6a	21n

Leviticus

19:17-18	54-55

Numbers

5:6	32

Deuteronomy

34:5-6	18

I Samuel

16:6	17

II Kings

2:9-12	19

Psalms

1:1-3	46
5:5	47
8:4	37-39
12:1	47
18:25	47
19:4b-5	47
25:12	47
32:2	47
33:2	9
37:23-24	48-49
50:20	55
80:17	39
94:11	49
103	125
103:15-18	132
109:6-7	48
127:5	48
128:4	48
144:3	39
146:3	39

Proverbs

3:13	49
3:30	50–51
5:21	49
7:24	51
15:18	49
16:9	49–50
17:17	55
18:9, 24	55

Isaiah

19:16	138n
66:13	131

Jeremiah

50:37	138n
51:30	138n

Ezekiel

2:1	42
41–42	42
45–46	42

Daniel

7:13–14	40–41

Nahum

3:13	138n

Malachi

4:4	19

NEW TESTAMENT

Matthew

5:13	32
5:31–32	138–139
8:20	19
10:35	32
14:21	138n
15:38	138n
16:13–20	101
19:10	32
23:8	58
25:31	41

Mark

1:17	32
3:35	55
9:2–4	20
16:4	19

Luke

2:1–20	117
9:19	19
10:25–37	55
17:1, 3	57–58

John

1:51	42
3:13	42
3:14	42
5:27	42
6:62	42
8:28	42
12:23	42
12:34c	42
13:31f	42
14:26	22–23, 32
16:21	32

Scripture Index

Acts

1:16	58
4:4	138n
6:3	58
7:56	41
21:7	58
28:14, 15	58

Romans

4:3	17
8:22–23	134
8:29	59–60
8:38–39	59–60
10:8–9	113–114

I Corinthians

6:5–6	56–57
11:3-16	8
11:23–25	72
12:3	113
14:34-35	8
15:21	32–33
16:13	138n

Galatians

1:2, 11; 2:4	61–62
3:6	17
3:7 & 9	34–35
3:28	59

Ephesians

5:22-24	8
6:10–17	101

Colossians

3:18	8

I Timothy

2:11-15	8
3:6	138n

II Timothy

4:7	138n

Hebrews

2:6–7	38–39

James

2:23	17

I Peter

2:9	24
3:1–6	8

Jude

Jude 9	20

Revelation

1:13	41
12:10	59
14:4	138n
14:14	41
19:10	59
22:3	126
22:9	59

Index of Personal Names

Abram (Abraham), 16–17
Aquinas, Thomas *See* Thomas Aquinas
Baring-Gould, Sabine, 100
Barth, Karl, 66
Beethoven, Ludwig, 75
Benson, Louis F., 77n, 80
Bonhöffer, Dietrich, 104
Bucke, Emory Stephens, 68n, 90n, 102n
Bullen, A. H., 114
Calvin, John, 9
Campbell, Antony F. , 29n
Carrier, Richard, 19n
Charlesworth, James H., 20n
Churchill, Sir Winston, 100
Clyde, Arthur G., 67n
Cordonnier, Deborah xvi, xix, 80n
Collins, Ace, 100n
Cyre, Susan, xvii, xix
Dalitz, Christopher, 72
Dearmer, Percy, 88n, 114n
Danton, Georges Jacques , 102
Duffield, George Jr., 101, 108
Eisenhower, President Dwight D., 100
Eco, Umberto, 65n
Elijah, 19
Enoch, 19
Euripides, 58
Fosdick, Harry Emerson 1
Gannett, William C., 89
Gilkeson, Florence, xx
Gruber, Franz, 111–112
Hadas, Moses, 5, 8n
Handel, George Friedrich, 9, 33
Higgs, Liz Curtis, 51
Hill, Anna White, xvi, xix, 126
Jacobs, Rep. Andy, 105
Jesse, 17
Jesus, 19–20, 37–39, 42, 115, 119, 139

Josephus, 20–21
Judah, Daniel ben, 87
Julian, John, 68n, 97n, 117n
Kilpatrick. James, 105n
Landsberg, Max, 89–99
London, Jack, 81
Lot, 15–16
Luther, Martin, 76
Lyon, Meyer, 87–88, 90
Lyte, Henry Francis, 127–36
Maimonides, Moses, 87
McIntosh, Peggy, 4n
McKim, LindaJo, 67n
McMahon, Maggie, xvi, xix
Mann, Newton, 89–99
Mohr, Josef, 111–12
Montgomery, James, 116–17, 119
Moulton, J. H., 22n
Moses, 18–21
Novitsky, Mary, xx
Olivers, Thomas, 87–98
O'Brien, Mark A., 29n
Ott, Dan, xix
Otto, Rudolph, 77
Patton, General George, 102
Paul, 24–35, 56, 59–60
Penelope, Julia, 3
Peter, 101
Polack, W. G., 112n
Ray, Richard A., xvii, xix
Roberts, Kathryn L., 126n
Samuel, 17
Saul, 17
Schiller, Friedrich, 75
Schutt, William H., vii, 9
Seiss, Joseph A., 68–72
Slusser, Jan, xix
Slusser, Jim, xix

Sorge, Sheldon, 65
Strong, James, 21n
Sullivan, Sir Arthur S., 100
Sydnor, James, 76n
Thomas Aquinas, 65
Truss, Lynn, 1, 92
Twain, Mark, 2
van Dyke, Henry, xvi, 75–85
Watts, Isaac, 95n, 109, 120
Wells, Amos R., 109n
Wesley, Charles, 102–3, 106–7
Wesley, John, 88, 104, 131
Willis, Richard Sotorrs, 68
Wink, Walter, 43n
Young, John Freeman, 111, 114

www.ingramcontent.com/pod-product-compliance
Lightning Source LLC
Chambersburg PA
CBHW062003180426
43198CB00036B/2148